TERTULLIAN
TREATISES ON MARRIAGE AND REMARRIAGE

TO HIS WIFE
AD UXOREM

AN EXHORTATION TO CHASTITY
DE EXHORTATIONE CASTITATIS

MONOGAMY
DE MONOGAMIA

Ancient Christian Writers

THE WORKS OF THE FATHERS IN TRANSLATION

EDITED BY

JOHANNES QUASTEN, S. T. D.
*Professor of Ancient Church History
and Christian Archaeology*

JOSEPH C. PLUMPE, Ph. D.
*Professor of Patristic Greek
and Ecclesiastical Latin*

The Catholic University of America
Washington, D. C.

No. 13

TERTULLIAN
TREATISES ON MARRIAGE AND REMARRIAGE

TO HIS WIFE
AN EXHORTATION TO CHASTITY
MONOGAMY

TRANSLATED AND ANNOTATED

BY

WILLIAM P. LE SAINT, S.J., S.T.D.

Professor of Theology
West Baden College
West Baden Springs, Indiana

NEWMAN PRESS

New York, N.Y./Ramsey, N.J.

Imprimi Potest:

>Joseph M. Egan, S.J.
>>*Praepositus Provincialis Prov. Chicagiensis*
>>*die 21 Maii 1951*

Nihil Obstat:

>Johannes Quasten
>>*Censor Deputatus*

Imprimatur:

>Patricius A. O'Boyle, D.D.
>>*Archiepiscopus Washingtonensis*
>>*die 8 Maii 1951*

Library of Congress
Catalog Card Number: 78-62462

ISBN: 0-8091-0149-1

PUBLISHED BY PAULIST PRESS
Editorial Office: 1865 Broadway, New York, N.Y. 10023
Business Office: 545 Island Road, Ramsey, N.J. 07446

PRINTED AND BOUND IN THE UNITED STATES OF AMERICA

CONTENTS

v

Contents

PAGE

TERTULLIAN
TO HIS WIFE

INTRODUCTION

The three treatises on marriage translated in the present volume, though not generally classified among Tertullian's major compositions, are works of considerable interest and importance. Patrologists and students of the history of dogma have long recognized their value as aids in tracing the gradual deterioration of his thought from Catholic orthodoxy to the harsh extremes of fanatical Montanism.[1] The professional theologian finds here source material which, with certain judicious reservations, can be used in support of the argument from tradition for theses on such vital subjects as the sacramental nature of marriage, the Church's jurisdiction over the marriage of Christians, the indissolubility of the contract-bond. Specialists in other fields are acquainted with passages in these works touching on questions of ecclesiastical discipline, moral problems, and liturgical practices which do much to clarify and illustrate the Church's code and cult at a very early period in Christian antiquity.

It is probably safe to say that for the general reader, perhaps even for most specialists, there is greater interest in single chapters, in individual paragraphs and sentences, than there is in the central thesis which these treatises develop and defend. In a true sense the parts here are of greater significance than the whole. For the theme of all three compositions is one which seems to have little pertinence today. Tertullian is concerned with the subject of second marriage. May a Christian man or woman remarry after the death of a consort? In the treatise addressed *To His Wife* he advises

3

against it, although he admits that to remarry is no sin.[2] In the *Exhortation to Chastity* his earlier counsel has already become an uncompromising command, while in the work on *Monogamy* he speaks of all second marriage as adultery, and attacks, with savage violence, the "sensualists" and "enemies of the Paraclete" who justify it by appeals to Holy Scripture and especially to the authority of St. Paul. Thus, what should be a matter of personal preference or personal ideals is made a matter of conscience; ascetical is confused with moral theology, discipline with doctrine; and a way of life which in some circumstances is of value to some individuals becomes a strict and essential obligation imposed upon all Christians. It is well to remind ourselves that such warped and exaggerated views were not the views of Catholics. They were heretical errors and were condemned by the Church as heretical, along with similar excesses in the direction of an unnatural rigidism propounded by Marcionites, Manicheans, Priscillianists, and other avowed enemies of sex and marriage.

This is not to say that the early Church looked favorably upon second marriage. Her attitude was the attitude of St. Paul,[3] one of toleration, not encouragement. In the face of a carnal world, it seemed much more consistent with her mission to encourage temperance, moderation, self-control, abnegation, asceticism; and if her asceticism seems misguided and severe by modern standards, we may be helped to understand it by reflecting that it was, at least in part, a reaction of disgust at the degrading licentiousness of her pagan surroundings. A detailed history of this question need not be given here. For the purpose of an introductory note it is sufficient to say that the general sentiment of the early Church was in favor of the legitimacy and against the propriety of second marriage;[4] the Montanist error lay in denying both propriety and legitimacy.

It is evident, then, that to know Tertullian the Montanist it is necessary to know his treatises on marriage. In fact, they epitomize the changing course, just as they reflect the changing temper, of his whole Christian life; for he wrote the *Ad uxorem* as a Catholic, the *De exhortatione castitatis* during a period which patrologists call one of semi-Montanism, and the *De monogamia* after his final, definite break with the Church. Of course, other points were at issue between Catholics and Montanists besides the dispute over second marriage. They were divided on such questions as the obligation of accepting ecstatic revelations as authentic manifestations of the Holy Spirit; the nature, number, and severity of the fasts to be imposed upon the Christian community; the sinfulness of flight during times of persecution; the priesthood of the laity; the Church's use of her power to forgive sins. We cannot say, then, that Tertullian's views on second marriage were decisive in making him a Montanist, but there can be no doubt that they contributed materially to his defection from the Church. Both St. Augustine[5] and St. Jerome,[6] in speaking of his heresy, state specifically that it consisted in a denial of the legitimacy of second marriage, an error which, they insist, is manifestly opposed to the teaching of St. Paul.

TO HIS WIFE

The treatise *Ad uxorem* is easily the best of Tertullian's three works on marriage. It is divided into two parts. In the first, he urges his wife to remain a widow if he should die before her. She is free to remarry, should she so wish, but she ought to consider the weighty reasons which advise against it. In brief, and roughly in order these reasons are: 1) marriage is good, but continence is better; 2) the polygamy of the Patriarchs is no argument in favor of multiple marriage; 3) St. Paul clearly shows his disapproval of second marriage; 4) it is concupiscence, manifested in a variety of ways, which impels people to marry a second time — and Christians should resist concupiscence; 5) the example of the saints encourages us to lead a life of continence; 6) even some pagans esteem and practice chastity; 7) when God separates husband and wife by the death of one or the other, He indicates His will that they remain single; 8) the Church shows her mind on the subject by not admitting digamists to the episcopacy.

These are Tertullian's principal arguments; along with them he uses many others which are subordinate and subsidiary. They are almost all repeated, in one form or another, but with much less moderation, in the *De exhortatione castitatis* and the *De monogamia*. Tertullian's policy in controversy is one of unremitting attack, with whatever weapons he has at hand — good or bad. As a result, while he is always vigorous, he is not always convincing,[7] and even readers who might be sympathetic to the thesis he here advances can hardly be favorably impressed by all of the arguments he uses in attempting to establish it. There are paralogisms on every page, and interpretations of Scripture which are either naive misapprehensions or tendentious distortions of its sense. It has been said that Tertullian was a good logician but a poor casuist.[8] This is a perspicacious appraisal, yet readers who examine the case he makes out against second marriage will see much more reason to concur with the latter estimate of his abilities than with the former.

The second half of the treatise deals with the subject of mixed marriage[9] and, in its essentials, it is as relevant today as it was eighteen hundred years ago. Tertullian begs his wife, if she does remarry, to make certain that she marries *in the Lord*, that is to say, that she marries another Christian. He shows that this is according to the teaching of the Apostle and points out, in a number of graphic illustrations, the difficulties and dangers which are involved in marriage with a person not of the faith. This section of his work, in spite of its almost inevitable exaggerations, is one of great interest and value. "Perhaps no monument of ecclesiastical antiquity portrays so well or so completely the whole manner of domestic life among ancient Christians."[10] The second section of the *Ad uxorem* contains passages of real beauty and concludes with an appreciation of Christian marriage which is unsurpassed in patristic literature.

It must be admitted, however, that Tertullian is a very difficult author to read—in English as well as in Latin—and it is possible that some who know nothing of his work, apart from a few popular phrases, may be disappointed when they come to grips, for the first time, with his paragraphs. The treatise *Ad uxorem* is fairly typical of his style. He is, paradoxically, at once concise and involved, brilliant and obscure.[11] There are passages here, as in almost all his works, which, except in paraphrase, produce no effect on the mind beyond what an eminent classicist once called "sheer paralysis."[12] Tertullian has a gift for words rather than sentences and it is much easier to appreciate his sallies than it is to follow his arguments. Perhaps this is why he is so often quoted and so infrequently quoted at length. He is, in spite of his defects, a truly great writer; there will be few to quarrel with the judgment of almost all present-day patrologists that he is the greatest in the West before Augustine.

The extant writings of Tertullian were composed during a period of literary activity which lasted for about twenty-five

years, from c. 197 to c. 222 A. D. It is generally agreed that
the *Ad uxorem* is to be dated some time between the years
200 and 206 A. D. Harnack argues[13] that it was probably
written when Tertullian and his wife were still in the prime
of life, since it was evidently composed before his lapse into
Montanism, and this took place, as we know, when he
reached middle age.[14] Moreover, he addresses his wife in
terms which show that he must have had some reason for
thinking that she would be able, without too much difficulty,
to marry again after his death. There seems to be little point
in attempting to date the composition more definitely than
this. We can be fairly certain that it was not written long
after the year 200 A. D. Tertullian was born between 150
and 160 A. D. Thus, if he composed the treatise in the year
200 A. D., it would have been written when he was about
forty or fifty years of age. This might still be called the prime
of life, which, happily, is not too restricted, either in meaning
or duration. However, it does approach pretty close to what
we must think of as a *terminus post quem non* in speaking
of middle age, even middle age in the life of a man who, as
St. Jerome says, *fertur vixisse usque ad decrepitam aetatem.*[15]

✦ ✦ ✦

The translation is based on A. Kroymann's text in volume
70 of the *Corpus scriptorum ecclesiasticorum latinorum*
(Vienna 1942) 96-124.[16] Occasionally, however, earlier
readings have been preferred, especially those of F. Oehler,
Quinti Septimii Florentis Tertulliani quae supersunt omnia
1 (Leipzig 1853) 667-97.

Two English translations of the *Ad uxorem* were made in
the last century: C. Dodgson, *Tertullian* 1 (LF 10, Oxford
1842) 409-431, and S. Thelwall, *Tertullian* (ANF 4, Amer.
repr., New York 1925) 39-49. These are both long out of

date and, in many difficult passages, quite meaningless. However, they have been consulted regularly and, at times, profitably. So also has K. A. H. Kellner's translation, to be found in his *Tertullians ausgewählte Schriften* 1 (BKV 7, Kempten-Munich 1912) 383-410. John Hoper's translation of the second book of the *Ad uxorem* (London 1550) was not available.

BOOK ONE

A SPIRITUAL LEGACY

I thought it would be well, my dearest companion in the service of the Lord, to give some consideration, even at this early date, to the manner of life that ought to be yours after my departure from this world, should I be called before you. I trust your own loyalty to follow the suggestions I shall offer. For if we pursue our purposes with such diligence when worldly issues are at stake, even drawing up legal instruments in our anxiety to secure each other's interests, ought we not to be all the more solicitous in providing for the welfare of those we leave behind us when there is question of securing their best advantage in matters concerning God and Heaven? Ought we not, acting as it were before the event,[1] bequeath them legacies of loving-counsel, and make clear our will respecting goods which constitute the eternal portion of their heavenly inheritance? God grant that you may be disposed to receive in its entirety the loving-counsel I now commit in trust to your fidelity. To Him be honor, glory, splendor, grandeur, and power, now and forever.[2]

This charge, then, I lay on you — that, exercising all the self-control of which you are capable, you renounce marriage after I have passed away. You will not, on that account, confer any benefit on me, apart from the good you do yourself. I would not want you to think that I now advise you to remain a widow because I fear to suffer hardship if you fail to preserve your person inviolate for myself alone. No, when the future time arrives, we shall not resume the gratification of unseemly passion. It is not such worthless, filthy things that God promises to those who are His own. More-

over, there is no promise given Christians who have departed
this life that on the day of their resurrection they will be
restored once more to the married state. They will, it is
clear, be changed to the state of holy angels.³ For this reason
they will remain undisturbed by feelings of carnal jealousy.
Even that woman who was said to have married seven
brothers in succession, will give no offense to a single one
of all her husbands when she rises from the dead; nor does
a single one of them await her there to put her to the blush.
The teaching of our Lord has settled this quibble of the
Sadducees. Yet it is still permitted us to consider whether
the course of action I recommend is of advantage to you
personally or, for that matter, to the advantage of any other
woman who belongs to God.⁴

MONOGAMY BLESSED BY GOD

2. Of course, we do not reject the union of man and
woman in marriage. It is an institution blessed by God for
the reproduction of the human race. It was planned by Him
for the purpose of populating the earth⁵ and to make pro-
vision for the propagation of mankind.⁶ Hence, it was permitted; but only once may it be contracted. For Adam was
the only husband that Eve had and Eve was his only wife;
one rib, one woman.⁷

Now, everybody knows that it was allowed⁸ our fore-
fathers, even the Patriarchs themselves, not only to marry
but actually to multiply marriages. They even kept concubines. But, although figurative language is used in speaking
of both Church and Synagogue,⁹ yet we may explain this
difficult matter simply by saying that it was necessary in
former times that there be practices which afterwards had
to be abrogated or modified. For the Law had first to inter-

vene;[10] too, at a later date, the Word of God was to replace the Law and introduce spiritual circumcision.[11] Therefore, the licentiousness and promiscuity[12] of earlier days—and there must needs have been abuses which called for the institution of a law—were responsible for that subsequent corrective legislation by which the Lord through His Gospel, and the Apostle in these latter days[13] did away with excesses or controlled irregularities.[14]

3. But I would not have you suppose that I have premised these remarks on the liberty which was allowed in former times and the severity of later legislation, because I wish to lay the foundation of an argument proving that Christ has come into the world for the purpose of separating those who are joined in wedlock and forbidding the conjugal relationship, as though from now on all marriages were to be outlawed. This is a charge they must be prepared to answer who,[15] among other perversions of doctrine, teach their followers to divide those who are *two in one flesh*,[16] opposing the will of Him who first subtracted woman from man and then, in the mathematics of marriage,[17] added two together again who had originally been substantially one. Finally, we do not read anywhere at all that marriage is forbidden; and this for the obvious reason that marriage is actually a good.

CELIBACY PREFERABLE TO MARRIAGE

The Apostle, however, teaches us what is better than this "good," when he says that he permits marriage, but prefers celibacy[18]—the former because of the snares of the flesh, the latter because the times are straitened. Hence, if we consider the reasons which he gives for each of these views, we shall have no difficulty in seeing that marriage is conceded to us on the principle that marry we may because marry we must.   But what necessity proffers necessity cheapens.[19] Scripture says that *it is better to marry than to burn*; but what sort of good, I ask you, can that be which is such only when it is compared to what is bad?[20]   Marriage, forsooth, is better because burning is worse!   How much better it is neither to marry nor to burn!

In time of persecution it is better to flee from place to place,[21] as we are permitted, than to be arrested and to deny the faith under torture.   Yet, far happier are they who find courage to bear witness and to undergo martyrdom for the faith.   It can be said that what is merely tolerated is never really good.   Suppose I am doomed to die.   If I quail at this, then it is good to flee.   If, however, I hesitate to use the permission given, this itself shows that there is something suspect about the very reasons for which the permission is granted.   Nobody merely *permits* that which is better, since this is something of which there can be no doubt; it is a thing which recommends itself by its own transparent goodness.[22]

Nothing is to be sought after for the sole reason that it is not forbidden.   When we come to think of it, even such things are, in a sense, forbidden because other things are preferred to them.   To prefer[23] the lofty is to exclude the low.   Nothing is good just because it is not bad, nor is it, therefore, not bad simply for the reason that it does you no hurt.   A thing that is good in the full sense of the word is to be preferred because it helps us, not merely because it does not harm us.   You ought to choose things that are good for you rather than things which are merely not bad for you.

Every contest is a straining for the first prize.   When a man comes out second, he has consolation, but he does not have victory. If we listen to the Apostle, then, *forgetting the things that are behind, let us stretch forth to those that are before,*[24] and be *zealous for the better gifts.*[25] Thus, although the Apostle does not *cast a snare upon us,*[26] he does show us where our advantage lies when he writes: *The unmarried woman . . . thinketh on the things of the Lord, that she may be holy both in body and in spirit. But she that is married is solicitous . . . how she may please her husband.*[27] In other places, also, the Apostle is nowhere so tolerant of marriage that he fails to point out his own preference, and this is that we strive to follow his example. Blessed is he who is like Paul![28]

THE WAY OF THE FLESH

4. But we read that *the flesh is weak;*[29] and this serves us as an excuse for pampering ourselves in a number of ways. We also read, however, that *the spirit is strong.*[30] Both statements are made in the same sentence.[31] The flesh is of the earth, the spirit is of Heaven. Now, why is it that, habitually seeking excuses for ourselves, we plead the weakness of our nature and disregard its strength? Should not the things of earth yield to the things of Heaven? If the spirit, being nobler in origin, is stronger than the flesh, then we have no one to blame but ourselves when we yield to the weaker force.

There are two weaknesses in human nature which appear to make it necessary that those who have lost a spouse should marry again. First, there is the concupiscence of the flesh, and this has the strongest pull; second, there is the concupiscence of the world. We servants of God[32] ought to scorn both weaknesses, since we renounce both lust and ambition.[33]

Concupiscence of the flesh urges in its defense the right to exercise the functions of maturity; [34] it seeks to pluck the fruits of beauty; it *glories in its shame*; [35] it declares that woman's sex requires a husband to be her strength and comfort, or to protect her good name from ugly gossip. But as for you, do you oppose against such specious arguments the example of those sisters of ours — their names are known to the Lord — who, having seen their husbands go to God, prefer chastity to the opportunities of marriage afforded them by their youth and beauty. They choose to be wedded to God. They are God's fair ones, God's beloved. With Him they live, with Him they converse, with Him they treat on intimate terms day and night. Prayers are the dowry they bring the Lord and for them they receive His favors as marriage gifts in return. [36] Thus they have made their own a blessing for eternity, given them by the Lord; and, remaining unmarried, they are reckoned, even while still on earth, as belonging to the household of the angels. Train yourself to imitate the example of continence furnished by such women as these and, in your love for things of the spirit, you will bury concupiscence of the flesh. You will root out the fleeting, vagrant desires which come of beauty and youth, and make compensation for their loss with the blessings of Heaven,which last forever.

THE WAY OF THE WORLD

The concupiscence of the world which I mentioned has its roots in pride, avarice, ambition, and the plea that one is unable to get along alone. [37] Arguments drawn from sources such as these it uses to urge the necessity of marriage; and, of course, it promises heavenly rewards in return: to queen it over another man's household; to gloat over another man's wealth; [38] to wheedle the price of a wardrobe out of another man's pocket; to be extravagant at no cost to yourself!

Far be it from Christians to desire such things as these! We are not solicitous about how we are to be supplied with the necessities of life — unless we have no confidence in the promises of God. He it is who clothes the lilies of the field in such great beauty; [39] who feeds the birds of the air, though they labor not; who bids us not to be concerned about the morrow, what we shall eat or what we shall put on. He assures us that He knows what is necessary for each of His servants. And this, certainly, is not a mass of jeweled pendants, nor a surfeit of clothing, nor mules brought from Gaul, [40] nor porters from Germany. Such things do lend lustre to a wedding, but what is necessary for us is, rather, a sufficiency which is consistent with sobriety and modesty. You may take it for granted that you will have need of nothing, if you but serve the Lord; indeed, all things are yours if you possess the Lord of all. Meditate on the things of Heaven and you will despise the things of earth. The widow whose life is stamped with the seal of God's approval has need of nothing — except perseverance!

5. In addition to the reasons already advanced, some say that they wish to contract marriage because they desire to live on in their posterity and because they seek the bitter sweet which comes of having children. To us this is sheer nonsense. For, why should we be so anxious to propagate children since, when we do, it is our hope — in view, that is, of the straitened times which are at hand [41] — that they will go to God before us. We ourselves desire, as did the Apostle, to be delivered from this wicked world and received into the arms of our Lord. [42]

Of course, to the servant of God posterity is a great necessity! We are so sure of our own salvation that we have time for children![43] We must hunt up burdens for ourselves with which, for the most part, even pagans refuse to be encumbered — burdens which are forced upon people by law,[44] but of which they rid themselves by resorting to murder of their own flesh and blood;[45] burdens, in fine,[46] which are especially troublesome to us because they constitute a danger to the faith. Why did our Lord prophesy, *Woe to them that are with child and that give suck,*[47] if He did not mean that on the day of our great exodus children will be a handicap to those who bear them? This is what comes of marriage. There will be no problem here for widows, however. At the first sound of the angel's trumpet they will leap forth lightly, easily able to endure any distress[48] or persecution, with none of the heaving baggage of marriage in their wombs or at their breasts.

THE CHRISTIAN WAY

Accordingly, whether marriage be for the flesh or for the world or for the sake of posterity, the servant of God is above all such supposed necessities. I should think it quite enough to have succumbed once to any one of them and to have satisfied all such wants as these in a single marriage.

Are we to have weddings every day and, in the midst of nuptials, to be overtaken by the day of dread, even as were Sodom and Gomorrha?[49] For in those places they were not just getting married and transacting business! When our Lord says that *they were marrying* and *they were buying*, He wishes to stigmatize those gross vices of the flesh and the world which most withdraw men from the things of God — the one by the sweet seduction of lust, the other by greed for gain. And yet, these men were afflicted by blindness of this kind at a time when the end of the world was still far off. How shall we fare, if the vices God then found detestable keep up back from divine things now?[50] *The time is short*, Scripture says; *it remaineth that they who have wives, act as if they had none.*[51]

6. But now, if those who actually have wives are to put them out of their minds, how much more are those who have none prohibited from seeking a second time what they no longer have! Accordingly, she whose husband has departed this life ought to refrain from marrying and have done with sex forever. This is what many a pagan woman does in order to honor the memory of a beloved spouse.

When something seems difficult to us, let us think of those who put up with difficulties greater than our own. For example, how many are there who vow virginity[52] from the very moment of their baptism![53] How many, too, who in wedlock abstain, by mutual consent, from the use of marriage! They have *made themselves eunuchs* because of their desire *for the kingdom of Heaven.*[54] If they are able to practice continence while remaining married, how much easier is it to do so when marriage has been dissolved! For I rather imagine it is more difficult to sacrifice something we actually have than it is to be indifferent about something we no longer possess.

EXAMPLES OF PAGAN VIRTUE

A hard thing it is, forsooth, and arduous, that a Christian woman, out of love for God, should practice continence after her husband's death, when pagans use the priestly offices of virgins and widows in the service of their own Satan! At Rome, for example, those women are called[55] "virgins" who guard a flame which typifies the *unquenchable fire*,[56] watching over that which is an omen of the punishment which awaits them together with the Dragon himself.[57] At the town of Aegium[58] a virgin is selected for the cult of the Achaean Juno; and the women who rave at Delphi do not marry. Further, we know that "widows" minister to the African Ceres, women whom a most harsh insensibility has withdrawn from married life.[59] For, while their husbands are still living, they not only separate from them but even introduce new wives to take their place — no doubt with the cheerful acquiescence of the husbands themselves! Such "widows" deprive themselves of all contact with men, even to the exclusion of kissing their own sons. Yet they become used to this discipline and persevere in a widowhood which rejects even those consolations which are found in the sacred bonds of natural affection. This is what the devil teaches his disciples. And they obey! As though on equal terms, the chastity of his followers challenges that of the servants of God. The very priests of Hell are continent.[60] For Satan has discovered how to turn the cultivation of virtue itself to a man's destruction, and it makes no difference to him whether he ruins souls by lust or chastity.

VARIOUS ARGUMENTS AGAINST SECOND MARRIAGE

7. We have been taught by the Lord and God of salvation that continence is a means of attaining eternal life, a proof of the faith that is in us, a pledge of the glory of that body which will be ours when we put on the garb of immortality,[61] and, finally, an obligation imposed upon us by the will of God.[62] Regarding this last statement, I suggest that you reflect seriously on the following: if it is a fact that not a leaf falls to the ground unless God wills it, then it is

equally true that no man departs this life unless God wills it. For it is necessary that He who brought us into the world should also usher us forth from it. Therefore, when God wills that a woman lose her husband in death, He also wills that she should be done with marriage itself. Why attempt to restore what God has put asunder? Why spurn the liberty which is offered you by enslaving yourself once more in the bonds of matrimony? *Art thou bound in marriage?* Scripture says, *seek not to be loosed. Art thou loosed from marriage? seek not to be bound.*[63] For, though *you sin not* in remarrying, yet, according to Scripture, *tribulation of the flesh will follow*[64] if you do.

Hence, as far as such a sentiment is possible, let us be grateful for the opportunity offered us of practicing continence and let us embrace it immediately, once it is offered. Thus, what we were unable to do in marriage we will be able to do in bereavement. We ought to make the most of a situation which removes what necessity imposed.

The law of the Church and the precept of the Apostle show clearly how prejudicial second marriages are to the faith and how great an obstacle to holiness. For men who have been married twice are not allowed to preside in the Church[65] nor is it permissible that a *widow be chosen* unless she was the wife of but one man.[66] The altar of God must be an altar of manifest purity[67] and all the glory which surrounds the Church is the glory of sanctity.[68]

The pagans have a priesthood of widows and celibates — though, of course, this is part of Satan's malevolence; and the ruler of this world, their *Pontifex Maximus*, is not permitted to marry a second time.[69] How greatly purity must please God, since even the Enemy affects it![70] He does this, not because he has any real affinity with virtue but because it is his purpose to make a mockery of what is pleasing to the Lord God.

DIGNITY OF CHASTE WIDOWHOOD

8. There is a brief saying, revealed through the mouth of the prophet, which shows how greatly God honors widowhood: *Deal justly with the widow and the orphan and then come and let us reason together, saith the Lord.*[71] The two groups mentioned here have no human means of support whatever; they are dependant on God's mercy, and the Father of all takes it upon Himself to be their protector. See how familiarly the widow's benefactor is treated by God! In what esteem, then, is the widow herself held when he who is her advocate will *reason with* the Lord! Not even to virgins themselves, I fancy, is so much given.

Although virgins, because of their perfect integrity and inviolate purity, will look upon the face of God most closely, yet the life a widow leads is the more difficult, since it is easy not to desire that of which you are ignorant and easy to turn your back upon what you have never desired.[72] Chastity is most praiseworthy when it is sensible of the right it has sacrificed and knows what it has experienced. The condition of the virgin may be regarded as one of greater felicity, but that of the widow is one of greater difficulty; the former has always possessed the good, the latter has had to find it on her own. In the former it is grace which is crowned, in the latter, virtue. For some things there are which come to us from the divine bounty, and others we have of our own efforts. Those which are bestowed upon us by the Lord are governed by His generosity; those which are achieved by man are won at the cost of personal endeavor.[73]

SAFEGUARDS OF CHASTITY

Therefore, cultivate the virtue of self-restraint, which ministers to chastity; cultivate industry, which prevents idleness; temperance, which spurns the world. Keep company and converse worthy of God, remembering the quotation sanctified by the Apostle: *Evil associations corrupt good manners.*[74] Chattering, idle, winebibbing, scandalmongering women do the greatest possible harm to a widow's high resolve. Their loquaciousness leads to the use of words offensive to modesty; their slothfulness engenders disloyalty to the austere life; their tippling issues in every sort of evil and their prurient gossip is responsible for inciting others to engage in the lustful conduct which such talk exemplifies. No woman of this kind can have anything good to say about monogamy. *Their god is their belly*, as the Apostle says; and so also is that which lies adjacent to it.[75]

Here, then, my dearest fellow servant, is the counsel which even now I leave with you. And, really, although my words are superfluous after what the Apostle has written on the subject, yet for you they will be words of consolation as often as, in thinking on them, you think of me.

BOOK TWO

MARRIAGE IN THE LORD

I have just finished describing, as well as I could, my dearest companion in the service of the Lord, the manner of life a Christian woman should embrace when, for one reason or another, her marriage is brought to an end. Now, recognizing the fact of human frailty, let us turn our attention to an alternative course of action. We are led to do this because of the conduct of certain women who, when given an opportunity of practicing continence by reason of a divorce [76] or the death of a husband, not only rejected the opportunity of living so good a life, but, in contracting a second marriage, were not even mindful of the prescription that they should *above all marry in the Lord.* [77]

As I write these words I am disturbed at the thought that I, who but recently exhorted you to practice monogamy and remain a widow, may be responsible, by my mere mention of marriage, for making you disposed to give up the higher ideal. Still, if you are truly wise, you will see clearly that you ought to lead the kind of life which is the best for you. It is because this ideal is so lofty, so difficult, and so exacting that I have tempered, to some extent, my remarks on the subject. I would have had no reason at all to bring up the matter, were it not for a very serious consideration which has engaged my attention. [78]

The continence which makes possible a life of widowhood is something heroic, and therefore it would seem that a woman can be all the more easily pardoned if she does not persevere in such a state. Failure is easy to excuse wherever

23

success is difficult to achieve. But to *marry in the Lord* is well within our power, and so failure here means that our guilt is the greater for our having neglected a duty which we are able to fulfill.

There is also this added consideration: when the Apostle writes that widows and virgins should *so continue*,[79] his language is that of persuasion, since he says, *I wish all to persevere according to my example.* But when there is question of marrying in the Lord, and he writes *only in the Lord*,[80] he no longer advises, he expressly commands. Disobedience, especially in a matter of this kind, is dangerous. For although a suggestion may be ignored with impunity, an order may not, since the former is a counsel proposed for our free choice, while the latter is a prescription of authority imposing a definite obligation. In the first instance we are guilty of indiscretion; in the second, of insubordination.

THE APOSTLE CONDEMNS MIXED MARRIAGE

2. Accordingly, when a certain woman recently married outside the Church,[81] taking a pagan for her husband, and when I recalled that this same thing had been done by others before her, I was astonished that women could be so wanton — or their spiritual directors so recreant. There is no authorization in Scripture for conduct of this kind. Can it be, I ask, that such persons justify themselves by an appeal to that chapter in First Corinthians where it is written: *If any brother hath a wife that believeth not and she agrees to the marriage, let him not put her away; in like manner a woman who is of the faith and married to a man that believeth not, if she finds that her husband is agreeable, let her not put him away; for the unbelieving husband is sanctified by the believing wife and the unbelieving wife is sanctified by the believ-*

ing husband, otherwise your children should be unclean?[82] This directive, which is meant for those of the faith who are actually married to pagans, they understand, possibly, in an unrestricted sense, as also conveying permission to contract marriage with pagans.[83]   God grant that those who interpret the text in this way are not practicing deliberate self-deception!

For it is obvious that Scripture in this place has reference to those Christians who were won to the faith by the grace of God after they had already contracted a pagan marriage. Take the words as they stand.   It says: *If any brother hath a wife that believeth not.* It does not say: *taketh a wife that believeth not.* This shows that a man who is already married to a pagan woman and who is afterwards converted by the grace of God, ought to continue to live with his wife.   The statement is made because otherwise such a convert might think that he is under the obligation of separating from a woman who is now become a stranger to him and, in a manner of speaking, no longer truly his wife.   A further reason is added when it is stated that *we are called in peace by* the Lord *God*[84] and that the marriage, if continued, may result in the pagan spouse being won to the faith by the Christian.   Moreover, the conclusion of this passage brings confirmatory proof that this is to be so understood; it reads: *As each is called by the Lord, so let him persevere.*[85]   It is the pagans who are called, I take it, not the faithful.[86]

If St. Paul had been speaking without qualification of a believer *prior* to his marriage, it would follow that he permits Christians to wed indiscriminately. If this were actually what he permitted, he certainly would not have subjoined a statement so different from and so contrary to the permission thus granted, saying: *A woman is free after the death of her hus-*

band. She may marry whom she will, but only in the Lord.[87] Here, surely, there can be no doubt[88] about his meaning, for the precise point which might have been at issue is explained by the Holy Spirit.[89]   Lest the sense of the words, *she may marry whom she will,* be misconstrued, he adds, *only in the Lord;* that is, *in the name of the Lord,* which means, unquestionably, *to a Christian.*

That Holy Spirit, therefore, who prefers that widows and unmarried women *persevere* in chastity and who encourages us to imitate the example he has given us,[90] recognizes no legitimate way of contracting a second marriage except *in the Lord.*   Only when this condition is fulfilled does he allow the sacrifice of one's chastity.   *Only,* he says, *in the Lord.* That word *"only"* added authority to his prescription.   No matter how you pronounce it, no matter what tone you use, it is a weighty word.   It commands as well as advises; it prescribes as well as exhorts; it entreats as well as threatens.   It is in itself a whole sentence, sharp, concise, and eloquent in its very brevity.   Thus always speaks the voice of God, so that we may understand at once and at once obey.   For who could fail to understand that the Apostle foresaw the many dangers lurking here, all the harm done to the faith by the type of marriages he condemns, and that, before all else, he wished to prevent the flesh of infidels from polluting the bodies of the saints?

But here someone may object: "What difference is there between a man who[91] is converted by the Lord after he has already married a pagan, and one who was a Christian at an earlier date, that is to say, before his marriage?   Why need they not both have the same regard for the sanctity of their bodies?   Why is the one forbidden to marry a pagan wife and the other commanded to persevere in such a marriage?

If we are defiled by contact with unbelievers, why is it that the one is not required to break up his marriage, seeing that the other is obliged not even to contract such a union?" To this I shall reply, with the help of the Holy Spirit.[92]

In the first place, let me emphasize that the Lord much prefers that a marriage be not contracted at all than that, once contracted, it be dissolved.[93] For He commends continence, while divorce He absolutely forbids, except for adultery.[94] Therefore, the one man has the duty of preserving his marriage intact, while the other has the liberty of not marrying at all.[95]

Secondly, Scripture states that those who are converted while living in marriage with a pagan are not defiled, because their partners are sanctified along with them. If this is true, then doubtless those who become Christians before their marriage and later on take a pagan wife, are unable to sanctify her flesh since they were not married at the time of their conversion. The grace of God sanctifies things as it finds them.[96] Therefore, whatever could not be sanctified remains unclean; and whatever is unclean has no part in what is holy. It can do nothing except defile it out of its own filth and kill it.

DANGER TO FAITH AND MORALS

3. In the light of all this it is evident that Christians who enter into marriage with pagans commit a sin of fornication and are to be cut off completely from communion with the brethren, in accordance with the letter of the Apostle who says, *with such a one we must not even break bread.*[97] Will we make bold to present our marriage certificates *on that day*[98] before the tribunal of our Lord and claim that a union which He Himself forbade is a union properly contracted?

Is it not adultery that He prohibits? Is it not fornication? Does not one who marries a pagan *profane the temple of God*[99] and *make the members of Christ the members of an adulteress?*[100]

As I see it, *we are not our own but we have been bought at a price.*[101] And how great a price it is! The very blood of God! Therefore, when we dishonor our bodies, we directly dishonor God Himself. What, then, did that man mean who said that to marry a pagan is a fault, but a very small one?[102] Even prescinding from the fact that in this case the bodies of those who are the Lord's are violated, we know, from other considerations, that every voluntary offense against the Lord is a serious offense.[103] In proportion as the sin was easier to avoid, so will the burden of our guilt be greater for obstinately committing it.

Let us now call to mind the other dangers foreseen by the Apostle, or rather, the injuries done the faith which I referred to above.[104] These are injuries which affect not just the body; they do serious harm to the soul as well. For who could doubt that faith is weakened day by day through contact with a pagan? *Evil conversations corrupt good manners*: how much more will uninterrupted familiarity under the same roof do so? Every Christian woman is obliged to obey the will of God. Yet how can she serve two masters,[105] the Lord and her husband, especially when her husband is a pagan? If she obeys a pagan, her conduct will be pagan. She will display the beauty of her body, make a show of elaborate coiffures,[106] worldly elegance, seductive charms; she will openly flaunt the sordid secrets of marital intimacies which, among Christians, are respected as necessary functions of sex and performed with modesty and moderation, as under the eyes of God.

4. But let her take care how she discharges her duties to her husband. Her duties to the Lord she certainly cannot fulfill according to the demands of ecclesiastical discipline, since she has by her side a servant of Satan who will act as an agent of his master in obstructing the performance of Christian duties and devotions. Thus, for example, if a *station* is to be kept,[107] her husband will make an early appointment with her to go to the baths;[108] if a fast is to be observed, her husband will, that very day, prepare a feast; if it be necessary to go out on an errand of Christian charity, never are duties at home more urgent! Who, indeed, would permit his wife to go about the streets to the houses of strangers, calling at every hovel in town in order to visit the brethren? Who would be pleased to permit his wife to be taken from his side, when she is obliged to be present at evening devotions? Or, to take another example,[109] who would not be concerned when she spends the whole night away from the house during the Paschal solemnities? Who, without feeling some suspicion, would let her go to assist at the Lord's Supper, when such vile rumors are spread about it?[110] Who would suffer her to slip into prison to kiss the fetters of a martyr? Or, for that matter, to salute any one of the brethren with a kiss?[111] Who would allow her to wash the feet of the saints?[112] To ply them with food and drink? Who would permit her to desire such things—or even to think of them? If one of the brethren, in traveling, stops at her house, what hospitality will he receive in the home of a pagan? If anyone is in need of assistance, the granary and pantry are closed and locked.

A HOUSE DIVIDED

5. But let us suppose that a man is found who does tolerate our way of life without complaint. Right here, then, there is a sin, in that the heathen come to know about these practices of ours; [113] we are subject to the scrutiny of the ungodly, and it is only through their kindness that we are allowed to do our duty. If a man tolerates something, he must necessarily know about it; if it is concealed from him because he will not tolerate it, then we are never free from fear. Now, since Scripture demands both [114] that we serve the Lord in secret and without anxiety, it makes no difference which of these precepts you violate. If your husband be tolerant, he becomes privy to what you do; if he be intolerant, it means trouble for you when you evade him.

Do not, the Lord says, *cast your pearls before swine, lest they trample them and, turning upon you, destroy you also.*[115] Among your "pearls" count also the distinctive religious observances of your daily life. The more you attempt to conceal them, the more suspect they become and the more they arouse a pagan's curiosity. Do you think to escape notice when you make the Sign of the Cross on your bed or on your body? [116] Or when you blow away, with a puff of your breath, some unclean thing? [117] Or when you get up, as you do even at night, to say your prayers? In all this will it not seem that you observe some magic ritual? [118] Will not your husband know what it is you take in secret before eating any other food? [119] If he recognizes it as bread, will he not believe it to be what it is rumored to be? [120] Even if he has not heard these rumors, will he be so ingenuous as to accept the explanation which you give, without protest, without wondering whether it is really bread and not some magic charm?

Suppose there are those who tolerate all this: yet they do so only to trample on and scoff at women who believe. They keep their "secrets" as a weapon in reserve — I mean the charge that they are Christians — if ever their wives displease them. They practice tolerance because they intend to make the dowries of their wives the price of their silence, that is, by threatening to expose them to the scrutiny of a judge.[121] This is a thing a great many women failed to think about, but came to understand only after their property had been extorted from them or their faith had been destroyed.

THE CHRISTIAN WIFE IN A PAGAN WORLD

6. Moreover, the handmaid of God is kept constantly engaged in duties foreign to her calling.[122] She is occupied in them on all the holidays of demons, on the festal days of rulers. At the beginning of each year, on the first of every month,[123] the odor of incense will assail her. She will step forth from her home through a door trimmed with laurel and hung with lamps as though it were some newly opened house of public prostitution.[124] She will recline at table with her husband in clubs and often in taverns. She who served the saints in days gone by will minister to sinners now, and not infrequently. Will she not see in this a sentence of damnation passed upon herself before the time, as she waits on those whom she was meant to judge?[125] Whose hand will she seek to clasp in hers? Whose cup will touch her lips? What kind of song will her husband sing to her and she to him? Some piece, no doubt, which is popular in theatres and pot-houses, this she will hear, this she will surely hear, some song which sounds in the throat of the devil himself. Is there ever any mention of God? Is there any prayer to Christ? Where is there any quoting of the Scriptures to

stimulate the faith? [126]   Where is there consolation of the Spirit?   Where is the blessing of God?   All is foreign, all is hostile, all is damned — the work of the Evil One to procure the destruction of souls. [127]

THE SITUATION OF THE CONVERT

7.   Though it may be true that these same things surround women who were converted to the faith after their marriage to pagans, yet such have the excuse that they were already living in this state when God laid hold of them.   They are told to persevere; they are become saints and are given the hope of gain. [128]   If, then, a marriage of this kind is approved by God, why will it not also be a successful marriage, in spite of difficulties and anxieties and obstacles and defilements, since it already enjoys the patronage of divine grace, at least in part? [129]

Thus, for instance, when an infidel is called to the practice of heavenly virtue, by an act of the divine condescension, this very fact inspires a feeling of awe in the heart of the spouse who remains a pagan.   As a result, he will be less violent in his attacks on the faith, less threatening, less suspicious.   He has been brought into touch with the miraculous, [130] he has ocular evidence of the truth, he sees that his wife is changed into a better person and thus, through reverential awe, he himself becomes a seeker after God. [131]   So it comes about that men like this are rather easily won over, once the grace of God has brought them into contact with the faith.

It is quite a different thing, however, to go down into forbidden ways wantonly and of one's own accord.   Whatever does not please the Lord, most certainly displeases Him and is most certainly the work of the Evil One.   A proof of this is found in the fact that Christian women are acceptable to those pagans only who have ulterior motives.[132] Thus there are men who do not hesitate to seek out such women in order to ruin them, to rob them of their goods, to deprive them of their faith. Here, then, is the reason which ought to assure you that no marriage of this kind can turn out well: it is procured by the Evil One and damned by the Lord.

FURTHER ARGUMENTS AGAINST MIXED MARRIAGE

8. Let us now, scrutinizing,[133] as it were, the divine decrees, see whether this be rightly so. Is it not true that, even among the heathen, masters who are strictest and most careful to preserve right order forbid their slaves to marry into other households? This is because they do not want them to break bounds in their debauchery,[134] to neglect the performance of their duties and give over their master's property to strangers. Is it not also decreed that persons may be claimed as slaves who continue to cohabit with the slaves of another, after he has formally forbidden them to do so?[135] Are we to regard earthly laws as more severe than those of Heaven? Are pagan women who marry strangers to lose their liberty, while Christian women who unite themselves to the slaves of the devil suffer no change in the status they enjoy?

They will deny, I suppose, that the Master through His Apostle has formally prohibited their conduct.[136] But what is the reason for madness such as this? None other than that weakness of faith which always leads to a passion for the pleasures of this world. This is a thing found, for the most part, among the wealthy. For the richer a woman is and the more puffed up she is with her position as a great lady,[137] so much the more extensive an establishment does she require to fulfill her social obligations and to serve her as a kind of field in which her ambition may maneuver without restraint. Churches seem contemptible to women such as these. since they will hardly find a rich man in the house of God,[138] and, if they do, he will hardly ever be unmarried. What, then, are they to do? Where but from the devil will they get husbands able to maintain their sedans, their mules, the outlandishly tall slaves they need to dress their hair?[139] No Christian, I fancy, however wealthy he might be, would supply such things as these.

Just reflect, if you will, on the example which is given by the conduct of pagan women. A great many of them, even those of noble birth and blessed with wealth, unite themselves promiscuously with mean and base-born men whom they have found able to gratify their passions or who have been mutilated for purposes of lust.[140] Some give themselves to their own freedmen and slaves, disregarding public opinion, as long as they have men from whom they need fear no check on their licentiousness.

Shall a Christian woman be ashamed to marry one of her own faith just because he is in moderate circumstances, when actually she would be enriched by a husband who is poor? For if *the kingdom of heaven belongs to the poor*,[141] it does not belong to the rich; and thus a woman who is wealthy will be better off with a man who is not. She will receive a dowry ampler than her own from the goodness of one who is rich in God. Let her be on his level here below, since it may be that in Heaven she will not be his equal! Should she hesitate and investigate and speculate constantly whether a man will be a proper husband to receive her dowry, when God has entrusted him with His own treasures?

THE BEAUTY OF CHRISTIAN MARRIAGE

How shall we ever be able adequately to describe the happiness of that marriage [142] which the Church arranges, [143] the Sacrifice [144] strengthens, upon which the blessing sets a seal, [145] at which angels are present as witnesses, and to which the Father gives His consent? For not even on earth do children marry properly and legally without their fathers' permission.

How beautiful, then, the marriage of two Christians, two who are one in hope, one in desire, one in the way of life they follow, one in the religion they practice. They are as brother and sister, both servants of the same Master. Nothing divides them, either in flesh or in spirit. They are, in very truth, *two in one flesh*; [146] and where there is but one flesh there is also but one spirit. They pray together, they worship together, [147] they fast together; instructing one another, encouraging one another, strengthening one another. Side by side they visit God's church and partake of God's Banquet; side by side they face difficulties and persecution, share their consolations. They have no secrets from one another; they never shun each other's company; they never bring sorrow to each other's hearts. Unembarrassed they visit the sick and assist the needy. They give alms without anxiety; they attend the Sacrifice without difficulty; [148] they perform their daily exercises of piety without hindrance. They need not be furtive about making the Sign of the Cross, nor timorous in greeting the brethren, [149] nor silent in asking a blessing of God. Psalms and hymns they sing to one another, [150] striving to see which one of them will chant more beautifully the praises of their Lord. Hearing and seeing this, Christ rejoices. To such as these He gives His peace. *Where there are two together*, there also He is present; [151] and where He is, there evil is not.

These, then, are the thoughts which the Apostle in that brief expression of his [152] has left for our consideration. Recall them to your mind, if ever there should be need to do so. Use them to strengthen yourself against the bad example which certain women give you. In no other way than this are Christians permitted to marry — and, even if they were, it would not be the prudent thing to do.

AN EXHORTATION TO CHASTITY

INTRODUCTION

There is very little controversy nowadays[1] over the prob
lem of dating the *De exhortatione castitatis.*[2] It was written,
apparently, between the years 204 and 212 A. D., at a time
when Tertullian, although obviously in sympathy with Montanism, was not as yet a member of the sect nor a declared
opponent of the traditional teaching of the Church on any
significant point of doctrine or discipline. On the subject of
second marriage his attitude is not essentially different from
what it was a few years before in the first part of the *Ad
uxorem.* Some new arguments are proposed and some old
ones expanded, but his answer to the problem remains the
same: Christians should not remarry. Tertullian is more
intransigent, more opinionated in the way he argues his case,
but he has not yet come to consider the rejection of second
marriage an *articulus stantis vel cadentis Ecclesiae.*

In a number of significant passages the *De exhortatione
castitatis* illustrates Tertullian's growing tendency to endorse
other Montanist ideas. Thus, for example, he quotes (10)
with approval the words of the Montanist visionary, Prisca,
as the words of a "holy prophetess"; and, when he speaks
of the Church and the priesthood, his language suggests (7)
that he has in mind, as an ideal, the internal, unorganized
church of the Spirit rather than the visible, hierarchical
church of Christ. Yet nowhere does he attack the Church
with the bitterness which is so marked a characteristic of the
De monogamia, nor does he identify himself with the sec-
taries by the use of such expressions as *nostri* and *vestri, penes
nos* and *penes vos* or *eos,* expressions of partisanship which

39

are of frequent occurrence in all of his later compositions and which help to identify them as Montanist.

The treatise is addressed to a friend, evidently a fellow Catholic, who has recently lost his wife. Tertullian urges him not to remarry. In developing his exhortation he stresses an argument against second marriage based on what he considers the clear indication of God's will that such unions should be avoided. God tolerates second marriage, but the very fact that He merely *tolerates* it proves that His positive will excludes what His permissive will allows. All the evidence of Sacred Scripture, both in the Old and the New Testament, shows that the practice is to be rejected. The Apostle himself, speaking in the name of the Lord, reprobates it when he asserts, equivalently, that it is the lesser of two evils.

In the course of his argument, especially in his exegesis (9) of Matt. 5.28 and 1 Cor. 7.1, 32 f., Tertullian is led to speak of marriage itself in terms which are somewhat less than enthusiastic. He does not dare to condemn a way of life which God Himself has blessed, but he does appear to regret its necessity.[8] His attitude here is that of a man who accepts the will of God but who does not like it. He seems to feel that there is something essentially unclean in any union of the sexes. Such unions may be legalized by external forms but they remain, in themselves, ugly and degrading; they are "good" only by extrinsic denomination. According to this twisted viewpoint, marriage is nothing but legitimate debauchery; it is a legitimate abuse rather than a legitimate use; or, to express his thought more exactly, the distinction between "use" and "abuse" is meaningless when there is question of the sex relationship, since this is not something which is good in itself, or even indifferent. It is, at best, a bad means justified by a good end.

It must be pointed out that such a position is quite inconsistent with much that he wrote on the subject of marriage in other places. There are passages in the *Ad uxorem* which reveal an attitude towards marriage, especially Christian marriage, which is certainly more than one of grim acceptance or sour toleration.[4] Some of the most vigorous pages in his *Adversus Marcionem* are devoted to the refutation of ideas similar to those which he himself defends in the present treatise.[5] And in the *De anima* he declares explicitly that we are to revere nature and not to be ashamed of it; the married state is blessed, not cursed by God and there is nothing immodest except excess.[6] D'Alès puts the matter briefly and well when he writes: "Tertullien a beaucoup écrit sur le mariage, et sur aucun sujet il ne s'est tant contredit."[7]

✦   ✦   ✦

The texts used in preparing this translation are those of A. Kroymann, *Corpus scriptorum ecclesiasticorum latinorum* 70 (Vienna 1942) 124-52, and F. Oehler, *Quinti Septimii Florentis Tertulliani quae supersunt omnia* 1 (Leipzig 1853) 737-57.

The following translations may also be noted:

Kellner, K. A. H., *Tertullians ausgewählte Schriften* 1 (BKV 7, Kempten-Munich 1912) 323-46.
Thelwall, S., *Tertullian* (repr. in ANF 4, New York 1925) 50-58.

THREE DEGREES OF CHASTITY

I have no doubt, my dear brother,[1] that now, since your wife has gone before you in peace, you are thinking a great deal about the loneliness of the life you lead,[2] as you endeavor to recover your tranquillity of spirit. I feel sure, then, that you stand in need of counsel and advice. Of course, in a situation such as yours a man ought to hold colloquy with the faith that is in him and seek a solution to his problem in the strength of this same faith. Yet, since in a matter like this the urgency of the flesh influences our thinking and usually opposes faith before the bar of conscience, we have need of another counselor besides our faith to act as advocate against the importunities of the flesh. We shall resist these importunities without difficulty if we attend to what God positively wills rather than to what He merely allows. A man acts meritoriously when he does the will of God, not when he takes advantage of a permission which He grants.

Now, *the will of God is our sanctification.*[3] For He desires that we who are His *image* should also become His *likeness,*[4] in order that we may be holy as He Himself is holy.[5] He has arranged various degrees of perfection in the "good" of which I speak — I mean our sanctification — so that we may be able to achieve at least some one of them. The first degree is to live a life of virginity from the time of one's birth; the second, to live a life of virginity from the time of one's second birth, that is to say, one's baptism, either by the mutual agreement of husband and wife to practice continence in marriage or by the determination of a widow or widower not to remarry; the third degree is that of monogamy, which is practiced when, after the dissolution of a first marriage, one renounces all use of sex from that time on.[6]

The first degree is one of blessedness, because you have had no experience whatever of that from which you will wish later on to be free; the second degree is one of self-control because you reject with contempt something whose strength you know quite well; the third degree, that is, not to rewed after the death of one's spouse, besides the merit of self-control has also the merit of resignation to God's will. We practice this resignation when we do not yearn after what is taken away from us, regarding it as taken away by the Lord God Himself, apart from whose will not even a leaf drops from a tree nor a sparrow, worth but a single farthing, falls to the ground.[7]

SECOND MARRIAGE AND THE WILL OF GOD

2. What a beautiful spirit of resignation is found, for example, in the text: *The Lord gave, the Lord hath taken away; as it hath pleased the Lord, so is it done.*[8] And thus, if we marry again after God has *taken away* our marriage, quite obviously we set ourselves against God's will, since we wish to have something which He decided we should not have. For if it had been His will that we should have it, He would not have taken it away from us.[9]

But perhaps we may set this construction upon the will of God, that He decides we may again have what He has previously decided we should not have.[10] It is not consistent with good, sound doctrine to attribute everything to the will of God in this way. For we deceive ourselves in asserting that nothing at all happens unless God permits it to happen, if we understand this assertion to mean that we ourselves have nothing to do with the event. There is no such thing as sin if we claim that everything we do is done because God wills it. Thus this principle will make for the destruction of all right order and even for the destruction of God Himself, were His will the cause of what He does not will or if there were nothing at all which He does not will.

The fact of the matter is that just as He prohibits certain actions, sanctioning His prohibition even by the threat of eternal punishment—and He surely does not wish actions to be performed which He forbids and which offend Him—so also does He command that certain other things be done, which are according to His will. He places such actions to our credit and recompenses them with an eternal reward. Thus it follows [11] that even after we have learned from His precepts both what He does and what He does not desire, we still have a will of our own and a power of choosing the one rather than the other, according as it is written: *Behold, I have placed before you good and evil, for you have eaten of the tree of knowledge.*[12]

THE WILL OF GOD AND THE WILL OF MAN

We ought not, then, ascribe to God's will something which has been the object of our own free choice, since He who wishes the good does not wish evil, unless we are to say that He who rejects what is evil does not wish what is good. Accordingly, it is of our own volition that we choose what is evil against the will of God, who wishes what is good. And if you ask me whence comes this volition of ours by which we set our will against the will of God, I should reply that it comes from our own selves. Nor is this rashly said, if, indeed, Adam, the author of our race and of our fall, willed the sin which he committed; for you yourself must needs be like the father whose seed you are. The devil did not force on Adam the choice of sin, but merely supplied him with an object he might choose. The will of God entered in to make his choice a matter of obedience.[13]

So you also, should you disobey the Lord, who gave you the power of free choice along with His command, will, of your own volition, turn aside to what He does not desire. And you imagine that in acting thus you have been overcome by the devil, who, though he wishes you to make a choice against the will of God, does not actually cause you so to choose! For neither did he force our first parents to make their choice of sin. The contrary is true, since they were not acting against their own wills, nor were they ignorant of what it was that God did not want them to do. He certainly did not want a thing to be done which, if done, He had decreed should be punished by death.[14] Hence, there is just one thing the devil does, he makes trial of you to see whether you will choose what it is in your power to choose —if you will! But when you have once made your choice then he makes you his slave, not by actually having willed your choice for you, but by seizing upon the opportunity given him in the choice you made yourself.

GOD'S POSITIVE AND HIS PERMISSIVE WILL

3. Accordingly, since we alone have the power of making our own decisions and since in so doing we show how we are disposed towards God, by choosing or not choosing to do His will, it follows that we must reflect deeply and seriously on the will of God, even in matters which are not perfectly plain.

Now, we all recognize God's will when it is clearly manifest, but we ought also to understand precisely *how* it is His will when He makes it known to us.[15] For although it seems that certain things are according to the will of God, since He allows them, yet it does not immediately follow that every permission represents the simple and absolute choice of the one who grants it. A permission is never granted except in a spirit of indulgence. This indulgence, though it is not involuntary, is brought about to some extent by the person in whose favor it is granted, and thus it is a kind of unwilling volition, since it is the result of an external force which restricts liberty. Just consider what sort of voluntary act that is which has some other person as its cause!

Moreover, there is a second kind of mixed volition [16] which we must take into consideration. God wishes us to do certain things which please Him, things which are determined by the demands of discipline and in which His indulgence has no mitigating influence. Yet, if there are some things which He prefers, that is to say, things which He would *rather* have us do, can there be any doubt that we ought to act according to His preference? We should regard the things which He desires less as really not desired at all, since there are other things which He desires more. For in showing us what He would *rather* have us do, He nullifies what He desires less by what He desires more; and the more clearly He lets you see both, the more definitely He insists that you do what He would rather have you do. If, then, He shows you in this way that He wants you to follow His preferential will, there is no doubt that, should you fail to do so, you will be guilty of a kind of disobedience, since you reject what He prefers. When you do what He merely wills and despise what He preferentially wills, your choice is more offensive than meritorious. You are, in part, guilty of sin; [17] and in part, even though you do not sin, you do fail to merit. And is not one's very unwillingness to merit itself a sin?

Now, if a second marriage is contracted according to the will of God which is called His "indulgence," I deny that such a marriage is purely and simply according to His will since, in this case, His volition is influenced by a spirit of toleration. On the other hand, if it is contracted according to that will which has opposed to it the preferential will that we practice continence, then, as we have seen, the non-preferential will is nullified by the preferential will.[18]

BETTER TO MARRY THAN TO BURN

I have written this preface so that I may now go on to an explanation of the doctrine of the Apostle. In the first place, I think I will not be reckoned with the ungodly if I call attention to a remark which he himself makes, to the effect that when he grants permission for marriage he is acting according to his own judgment, that is, according to a human way of looking at things, and is not repeating a precept which he has from God.[19] For even after he explains that widows and those who are single should marry if they cannot practice continence, since *it is better to marry than to burn*, he turns to another class of persons and says: *But to them that are married, not I but the Lord giveth commandment.*[20] By indicating this change of subject from himself to the Lord, he shows that what he said before he said on his own authority and not on the Lord's, to wit, that *it is better to marry than to burn*.

Now this statement, though it refers exclusively to those who are single or living in widowhood at the time when they are converted to the faith,[21] is cited by all who wish to justify marriage for any reason whatever. Hence, I should like to make clear what sort of "good" that is which is suggested as better than the pain of a punishment, a "good" which cannot be viewed as such except when it is compared with the greatest of all evils, so that only in this relative sense is it good to marry — because it is worse to burn![22]

A thing deserves to be called "good" only if it is such in an absolute sense, without any reference, I do not say to evil, but even to another good, so that if it be compared with another good and found inferior, it remains, nevertheless, good in itself. But if we are obliged to call it "good" by comparison with something that is evil, then it is not so much a good as it is a kind of lesser evil. The predication "good" is a forced predication, because the true nature of the thing itself is obscured by the presence of a greater evil. Indeed, take away the term of comparison, so that you do not quote, *It is better to marry "than to burn,"* and then let me ask whether you would presume to say simply, *It is better to marry*, without indicating precisely what that is with respect to which marriage is better. Therefore what would no longer be better is not even good, because in removing the term of comparison which makes marriage out to be better than some other evil, you remove the element which constrains us to speak of it as good.

We ought understand, then, that *it is better to marry than to burn* in the same sense in which it is better to have one eye than none.[23] Once you get away from the term of comparison, you see immediately that it is not really better to have just one eye, since this itself is not a good.[24] Therefore, let no one seize upon this chapter in seeking to defend a position he has adopted. Strictly speaking, it has reference only to those who are single or living in widowhood, and thus not actually bound by marriage ties. Yet even these, as I hope I have shown, ought to understand the nature of the permission which is granted them.

ST. PAUL OPPOSES SECOND MARRIAGE

4. As we know, the Apostle, when he speaks of second marriage, says plainly: *Art thou loosed from a wife? Seek not a wife. But if thou take a wife, thou dost not sin.*[25] However, this statement also is introduced as a matter of personal opinion and is not based on any divine precept.

There is a big difference between a commandment given by God and a counsel given by man. *I have no commandment of the Lord*, he says; *but I give counsel, as having obtained mercy of the Lord, to be faithful.*[26] Neither in the Gospel nor in the epistles of Paul himself will you find any permission for second marriage based on a commandment of God's. This fact, then, confirms the conclusion that marriage is to be contracted only once, since we must acknowledge that a thing is forbidden by God when there is no evidence that He permits it.

Remember also that after Paul interposes this merely human counsel of his, he appears to recognize that he has spoken rather extravagantly and at once attempts to moderate and retract what he has allowed. He does this when he subjoins the words: *Nevertheless, such shall have tribulation of the flesh;* when he says that he *spares* them; when he adds that *the time is short* and that, therefore, *those who have wives should be as though they had none;* when he contrasts the solicitude of those who are married with the freedom of those who are not.[27] In using expressions of this kind, which show why it is better not to marry, he is advising against a course of action which before he had indulgently permitted. And if this is his attitude with respect to a first marriage, how much more will it be his attitude with respect to a second!

Again, when he exhorts us to follow his example, he indicates what he wishes us to be, and that is, continent. At the same time he acquaints us with what he does not wish us to be. So he also, since he desires one course of action rather than another, cannot be thought of as freely and unequivocally permitting something which has been shown to be against his will. If he truly desired it, he would have commanded it, not just permitted it.[28]

Well, but in the same chapter he declares that a woman *is at liberty to marry whom she will if her husband die, yet only in the Lord.* True enough, *but more blessed shall she be,* he says, *if she so remain, according to my counsel; and I think that I also have the Spirit of God.*[29] Here we have two counsels — the one, given first, in which he permits marriage; the other, coming later, in which he instructs us to remain continent. Which, then, you ask, should we accept? Study them closely and, after that, decide. In the one case, when he gives permission, he tells us that he is acting according to human wisdom; in the other, when he enjoins continence, he asserts that the advice he gives is according to the Holy Spirit. Do you follow the counsel which has God as its author.

It is true that all the faithful have the Spirit of God, yet they are not all Apostles. When, therefore, one who had said that he was among the faithful, stated later on that he had the Spirit of God — and nobody would deny that all the faithful have it — he made the assertion in order to prove that he had been raised to the apostolic dignity. For the Apostles have the Holy Spirit in their own special, personal way; not partially, as all others have, but fully, in prophecy, miracles, and the gift of tongues. Accordingly, St. Paul advances the authority of the Holy Spirit for that course of action which he himself preferred us to follow. Thus it is no longer a mere counsel of the Divine Spirit which is given us but, in view of His majesty, this counsel is a command.

MARRIAGE IN GOD'S PRIMEVAL PLAN

5. The very origin of the human race furnishes us with an argument for the law of monogamy, since it gives ample evidence of what God ordained in the beginning as a norm to be followed by future generations. For after He had

formed [30] man and saw that he must needs have a companion like himself, He took one of his ribs and made of it one woman, although obviously matter for others was not lacking nor was the Artisan unequal to the task of making more. Adam had many ribs,[31] and the hands of God are tireless; yet more wives than one God did not create. And, therefore, the man whom God made, Adam, and the woman whom God made, Eve, living in monogamy, fixed this as an inviolable law for mankind, a law based on God's original decree and the precedent set in the beginning.

Again, he says:[32] *They will be two in one flesh* — not three or four. If there were three or four they would not really be one flesh, nor two in one flesh. They will be such only if their union is formed once and for all.[33] But if they marry a second time, or oftener, their oneness no longer exists; there will not be two in one flesh, but, on the contrary, many in one.

When the Apostle interprets the text, *They will be two in one flesh*, in its relationship to Christ and the Church,[34] he is thinking of the spiritual nuptials between Christ and the Church, in which Christ is one and His Church is one. We must see in this a second promulgation of the law of monogamy, and an emphatic promulgation, since it derives not only from the primitive establishment of human society but also from Christ's own sacrament.[35] In both instances we draw our origins from a monogamous union, carnally through Adam, spiritually through Christ. There is one law of monogamy derived from these two nativities. In either case deviation from monogamy means degeneration.[36] Plurality of marriage began with a man accursed. Lamech was the first who, in espousing two women, made three in one flesh.[37]

THE POLYGAMY OF THE PATRIARCHS

6. And yet, you will say, the blessed Patriarchs contracted multiple marriages, not only with wives but even with concubines. Is it, then, not lawful for us also to marry repeatedly? Certainly, it is lawful, if your nuptials are types or symbols prefiguring something yet to come,[38] or if the ancient command, *increase and multiply*,[39] is still valid in our own day and not superseded by the warning that *the time is short*, that *it remaineth that they also who have wives act as if they had none*.[40] Actually, the precept of continence in this text, and the restriction placed on intercourse, which is the seeding of the race, have abolished the ancient command to *increase and multiply*. It is one and the same God, I take it, who ordains and disposes in both cases. It is evident that in the beginning He wished the race to be sown and, accordingly, gave full liberty in the matter of wedlock, until the earth should be *filled up*[41] and there should be reason for a different dispensation. But now, in these latter times,[42] He has restricted what He allowed before and revoked the indulgence which He had then permitted.

It is reasonable that restrictions should, in the end, replace early concessions. It is always at the beginning that things are lax. A man plants a wood and permits it to grow so that in due time he may cut it down. Let this stand for the old dispensation which is pruned by the new Gospel, wherein *the ax is laid to the root of the tree*.[43] So, also, the law of *An eye for an eye and a tooth for a tooth*[44] became the "old law" when *Let none return evil for evil*[45] became the "new."[46] And even among men I have an idea that the more recent enactments and decrees take precedence over those which have gone before.

THE PRIESTHOOD AND MONOGAMY

7. Speaking, however, of examples from times past, why do we not select those which have something in common with present discipline and which show points of contact between ancient usage and the law of our own day? For instance, I observe that the old law also curtailed the privilege of repeated marriage. The warning is given in Leviticus: "Let not my priests marry a second time."[47] I may say that that is a "second time" which is not once; and that which is not once is multiple, since after unity begins multiplicity. Everything which exists once for all is one.[48]

But it was reserved for Christ to bring about the fulfillment of the law,[49] in this matter as well as in others. Accordingly, then, with us the law which requires that none but monogamists are to be chosen for the order of the priesthood,[50] is more comprehensive in its scope and exacting in its details. So true is this that, as I recall, there have been men deposed from office for digamy.[51]

Well, then, you will say, it follows that all whom the Apostle does not mention in this law are free. It would be folly to imagine that lay people may do what priests may not. For are not we lay people also priests?[52] It is written: *He hath made us also a kingdom, and priests to God and His father.*[53] It is ecclesiastical authority which distinguishes clergy and laity,[54] this and the dignity which sets a man apart by reason of membership in the hierarchy.[55] Hence,[56] where there is no such hierarchy, you yourself offer sacrifice, you baptize, and you are your own priest. Obviously, where there are three gathered together, even though they are lay persons, there is a church.[57]

For, as the Apostle also says, each *man liveth by faith,*[58] *nor is there respect of persons with God,* since *not the hearers*

of the law are justified by the Lord, but the doers.[59] Therefore, if in time of necessity you have the right to exercise a
priestly power, you must also needs be living according to
priestly discipline even when it is not necessary for you to
exercise priestly powers.[60] As a digamist will you baptize?
As a digamist will you offer sacrifice? How much more
serious a crime[61] is it for a lay digamist to perform sacerdotal
functions, when a priest who becomes a digamist is removed
from his priestly office![62]

Yes, you will say, but allowance must be made in case
of necessity. The plea of necessity will not be allowed, if
the necessity itself need never have arisen. Therefore, do
not let yourself be found living as a digamist, and you will
not be placed under the necessity of performing such minis-
tries as are forbidden to a digamist. God wishes every one of
us to be ready at all times to administer His sacraments
properly. There is *one God, one faith*[63] — let there be one
discipline also. So true is this that we may well ask how we
shall ever obtain priests from among the laity, if laymen fail
to lead the kind of life demanded of those who are chosen
for the priesthood. Therefore, we must insist that the obligation of avoiding second marriage rests first of all on the
laity, since no man can become a priest except one who,[64]
as a layman, lived in monogamy.

NOT ALL THAT IS LICIT IS GOOD

8. Let us admit that second marriage is licit — if everything licit is good. It is the same Apostle who exclaims: *All
things are lawful, but not all things are expedient.*[65] Now I
ask you, can a thing which is not expedient be called "good"?
If even such things as are not salutary are lawful, then it follows that even things which are not good are lawful. What

course of action ought you choose to follow, one which is "good" because it is lawful, or one which is good because it is beneficial? There is quite a big difference, as I see it, between what is permitted and what is advantageous. When something is really a good we never say, "It is permitted"; for what is good presents itself as something to be embraced, not as something to be tolerated.

A thing is permitted only if there is some doubt whether it is good or not; the same thing may also be prohibited if there is no serious reason why it should be allowed. Thus, second marriage is permitted because of the danger of incontinence; for if permission were never granted to do something which is not good, it would be impossible to distinguish a man who submits to the will of God from one who follows his own freedom of choice, or a man who strives to do what he can [66] in order to promote his own best interests from one who embraces every opportunity of self-indulgence which is afforded him.

A permission is usually a test of character, because to resist temptation is to prove one's mettle, and because a permission is often itself a temptation. Thus it is, then, that *all things* may be *lawful, but not all are expedient,* since a man is subjected to a test when a permission is granted him and it is on the basis of this test in matters permitted that he is judged. Even the Apostles were permitted to marry and *to take their wives about with them.*[67] They were also permitted *to live by the Gospel.*[68] But he who did not use such rights [69] when the opportunity to do so was offered him, inspires us to follow his example, showing us that approval is to be won precisely there where a permission which is given us prepares the way for a test of self-control.

MARRIAGE AND CONCUPISCENCE

9. If we penetrate deeply into his thought, we shall have to say that second marriage is really nothing but a kind of fornication.[70] For when he asserts that married people make this their one concern — *how they may please*[71] each other — he is surely not referring to their practice of virtue, since he would not impugn a solicitude for things that are good. Rather he wishes it understood that they will be anxious about such things as clothes and jewels, completely given over to the pursuit of beauty, in seeking seductive charms. It is the genius of carnal concupiscence that it is able to arouse passion at the mere sight of a beautiful body richly adorned. This same concupiscence is the cause of fornication. Do you not think, then, that second marriage is of the same nature as fornication, since the evils we see in it are the same as those associated with fornication?

The Lord Himself says: *whosoever shall look on a woman to lust after her, hath already committed fornication with her in his heart.*[72] But does a man who looks on a woman with a view to marriage do anything more or less than this? Suppose he actually marries her. He would not do so if he had not first lusted to have her in marriage or looked at her in order to excite his lust — unless we are to suppose that a man can marry a woman whom he has never seen or for whom he has never felt any desire!

Now, everybody knows that it makes a big difference whether it is a married or an unmarried man who lusts after another woman. To an unmarried man every woman is "another woman" as long as he is not married to her, and the selfsame action which makes one woman a wife, makes another an adulteress.[73] Marriage and fornication are different only because laws appear to make them so; they are not intrinsically different, but only in the degree of their illegitimacy. For what is it that all men and women do in both marriage and fornication? They have sexual relations, of course; and the very desire to do this, our Lord says, is the same thing as fornication.[74]

But then, it is objected,[75] is not your doctrine destructive of all marriage, even monogamy? — Yes, and with good reason, since this, too, in the shameful act which constitutes its essence, is the same as fornication.[76] Therefore, *it is best for a man not to touch a woman.*[77] So, too, the most perfect sanctity is that of the virgin, because it has nothing in common with fornication. Furthermore, since arguments of this kind can be used to urge abstention from even a first and single marriage, how much more valid are they against contracting a second!

Be grateful if God has been so indulgent as to permit you to marry once. You will also have reason to be grateful if you do not act on the permission He has given you to do so a second time. If you fail here, you will abuse His indulgence, since you use it immoderately. "Moderation" comes from the word meaning "limit."[78] Is it not enough that you have slipped from the level of immaculate virginity to the level next beneath it by getting married? Indeed, once you have shown yourself incontinent in a second stage, you will fall lower and lower, to a third stage and a fourth and perhaps to others even farther down, since a man who has not hesitated to marry twice, thereby indicates his readiness to marry many times.

Shall we have weddings every day and in the midst of nuptials be overtaken by the last day, even as were Sodom and Gomorrha?[79] That day will the *woe* pronounced over *hem that are with child and that give suck*[80] be fulfilled,

over the married, that is, and the incontinent; for from marriage come swelling wombs and breasts and infants. And
when will there be an end of marrying? I suppose, when
there is an end of living!

THE BLESSINGS OF CONTINENCE

10. Let us renounce the things of the flesh so that we may
in due season bring forth fruits of the spirit. Make the
most of your opportunity to be free from one to whom you
must *render the debt* [81] and who must render it to you. This
may not be to your liking, but it is certainly to your best
interest. Your debtor days are over. O happy man! But
you have lost someone who was in debt to you. Suffer the
loss! Suppose you discover that what we call a loss is actually
a gain? Indeed, if you now practice continence, you will
amass a great store of sanctity. Deny the flesh and you will
possess the spirit.

As a proof of this, let us reflect on what our own experience
teaches us. How much better a man feels when he happens
to be away from his wife. He has a fine appreciation of
spiritual things. When he prays to the Lord, he comes close
to Heaven. If he applies himself to reading the Scriptures,
he is completely absorbed in them. If he sings a Psalm, he
sings with joy in his heart.[82] If he adjures a demon,[83] he
does so with confidence. It is for this reason that the Apostle
recommends periodic abstinence, so that we may be able to
pray more effectively.[84] He wishes us to realize that a policy
which is temporarily expedient ought to be made permanent,
so that it may be permanently expedient. Men need prayer
every day and every moment of the day; and if prayer is
necessary, so, also, of course, is continence.

It is our conscience which leads us to pray; if our conscience feels shame, we shall be ashamed to pray. It is our spirit which directs our prayer to God;[85] if our spirit has to accuse itself because of a guilty conscience, how will it dare place our prayer on God's altar, since, when our conscience is guilty, this holy minister, our spirit, is also put to the blush?

There is a prophecy in the Old Testament which reads: *You shall be holy because God is holy;*[86] and another: *With the holy Thou wilt be holy and with the innocent Thou wilt be innocent and with the elect, elect.*[87] We must walk worthily in the discipline of the Lord,[88] and not according to the unclean desires of the flesh. In line with this, the Apostle also says that *to be wise according to the flesh is death, but to be wise according to the spirit is life eternal*[89] in Christ Jesus our Lord. In like manner the holy prophetess Prisca[90] declares that every holy minister will know how to administer things that are holy. "For," she says, "continence effects harmony of soul, and the pure see visions and, bowing down, hear voices speaking clearly words salutary and secret."

THE FAITHLESS SPOUSE

11. But if spiritual insensibility, which results from the use of sex in even a single marriage, repels the Holy Spirit, how much more will this be the case if the practice continues in a second marriage! Here a man's reason for shame is doubled, since after a second marriage he has two wives by his side, one in the flesh, the other in the spirit. Your affection for your first wife will become even more devoted, now that she is secure in the Lord. You certainly will not be able to hate her. You pray for her soul.[91] You offer the annual Sacrifice for her.[92] Do you wish, then, to stand before the Lord with as many wives as you remember in your prayers? Will you offer the Sacrifice for two wives and have recom-

mendation made of both through the ministry of a priest whose monogamy is a necessary condition for his ordination, or who is consecrated for his office in a special way by reason of his virginity, and who stands at the altar surrounded by widows who were married only once? Will you feel no shame as your sacrifice ascends before the Lord? Will you dare ask chastity for yourself and for your wife, among the other spiritual gifts [93] you pray for?

THE SPECIOUS REASONING OF LUST

12. I know the pretexts which we allege in order to conceal our insatiable lust after the pleasures of the flesh.[94] We pretend that we need assistance in taking care of the house, controlling the domestics, keeping an eye on coffers and keys, supervising the spinning, managing the kitchen, sharing cares and responsibilities. I suppose that it is only in the houses of married men that things run smoothly! The households of bachelors, the estates of eunuchs, the fortunes of soldiers and men who travel abroad without their wives are all undone! Are not we Christians also soldiers? [95] Yes, and subject to a stricter discipline because soldiers of so great a Leader? Are we not also strangers in this world? [96] Why, then, O Christian, is your life such that you cannot lead it without a wife?

Granted now that a wife is necessary to help you bear the burden of domestic duties. Very well, you may have one, but take one who will be a kind of spiritual wife. Take one of the widows, one who is beautiful in faith, whose dowry is poverty, whose age is her adornment. Thus you will make a good marriage. You may even have many such wives, and please God withal.[97]

To think that Christians should be concerned about posterity — Christians for whom there is no tomorrow![98] Is a servant of God to hope for heirs, when he has disinherited himself from the world? If a man has no children in his first marriage, is this a reason for seeking a second? The first fruit of this will be that he will wish for a longer life — whereas the Apostle can hardly wait to go to God.[99] Doubtless, when persecutions come, a man in this position will be best prepared to meet them unencumbered. He will be the most steadfast under torture. He will show greatest restraint in acquiring wealth and the greatest generosity in sharing it with others. Finally, he will die without a care, since, perchance, he will leave sons behind him to perform, with due solemnity, the sacrifices at his grave![100]

Can it be that men like this act out of consideration for the commonwealth? Are they afraid that our cities will decline, along with the falling birthrate? Are they afraid that law and justice will be neglected, commerce destroyed, the temples abandoned? Are they afraid there will be no one to shout, "The Christians to the lion"?[101] This, actually, is what they wish to hear who are anxious to have children.

The fact that children are a troublesome burden, especially in our times, should be a sufficient argument for widows and widowers to remain unmarried.[102] Men have to be forced by law to father a family, because no man in his right senses would ever care to have children. But suppose that, in spite of this reluctance of yours, you do cause your wife to conceive. What will you do? Will you interrupt her pregnancy by the use of drugs?[103] I rather imagine that we have no more right to murder a baby before birth than after it. Perhaps, though, when your wife is pregnant, you will have the effrontery to ask that God relieve you of this great care, albeit you refused His relief when it was offered you.

I suppose that you will look around for some woman who is barren or who is at an age when passion is burned out. A wise course, truly, and one eminently Christian! For we do not believe, do we, that a sterile woman or one advanced in years has ever borne a child, when God so willed? [104] Such a thing is all the more likely to occur when a man tempts God by the presumption inherent in such worldly prudence. To give just one instance: I know a man, one of the brethren, who married a second time and, because of his daughter, took a "barren" woman: he promptly became a father again, as well as a husband!

THE CHALLENGE OF THE HEATHEN

13. I may add to this exhortation of mine, dear brother, certain examples given us by the pagans themselves. Such examples are often placed before our eyes for the value they have as testimonials to truth. This happens when something which is good and pleasing to God is recognized as such even by the heathen and honored by the evident regard they have for it. Thus, monogamy is so highly prized by the pagans that when a virgin is married according to the law, a woman who has been wedded only once must act as matron of honor. [105] If this is intended as an omen, it is certainly a good one. [106] In like manner it is required that at certain official celebrations and functions precedence be given a woman married only once; at all events, the wife of the *Flamen* must be married once only, and the same law applies to the *Flamen* himself; [107] and, of course, it is one of the glories of monogamy that not even the *Pontifex Maximus* [108] may marry a second time.

Now, then, when Satan imitates the divine mysteries, he issues a challenge to us. We ought, indeed, to be ashamed if we are slow to practice continence for God's sake, since others do it for the devil's sake, some in a life of perpetual virginity, others in perpetual widowhood. We know about the Vestal Virgins,[109] the virgins of Juno in a city of Achaea,[110] those of Apollo at Delphi, of Minerva and Diana in certain other places. We know about others, also, who live a celibate life: the priests of that famous Egyptian bull,[111] for example, and those women who, of their own accord, leave their husbands and grow old in the service of the African Ceres, renouncing forever all contact with men, even the kisses of their own sons. For the devil, after discovering the power of lust, has found out a chastity also with which to work perdition. A Christian, then, is all the more guilty if he refuses to embrace a chastity which effects salvation.

As witnesses to our argument we may mention also certain women who have become famous because of their devotion to the ideal of monogamy. A Dido,[112] for instance, fugitive in an alien land, should have been glad of the opportunity to marry a king. Yet, lest she be bigamous, she preferred "to burn" rather than "to marry."[113] And the renowned Lucretia, forced against her will to submit to the embraces of a man who was not her husband, and this but once, cleansed the defilement of her flesh by shedding her own blood, lest she be forced to live with the thought that she was no longer the consort of a single individual.[114] With a little effort you could illustrate this over and over again from the lives of our own women. Such examples will be better, too, than those I have already mentioned, since it is much more remarkable to live in chastity than it is to die for it. It is easier to lay down your life because you have lost something you valued than it is to keep on living in order to protect something for which you would gladly die.

CONCLUSION

How many men and women there are whose chastity has obtained for them the honor of ecclesiastical orders![115]   How many who have chosen to be wedded to God!   How many who have restored to their flesh the honor it had lost![116] They have already set themselves apart as children of the world to come by killing concupiscence and, with it, all else that has no place in Paradise.[117]   Therefore, we must conclude that those who wish to enter Paradise ought, at long last, to put an end to a way of life which is not found in Paradise.[118]

MONOGAMY

INTRODUCTION

The *De monogamia* is one of Tertullian's most notable contributions to the cause of militant Montanism. The arguments developed in the treatise are substantially the same as those which he used in the *Ad uxorem* and the *De exhortatione castitatis* to oppose the practice of successive polygamy; the great difference is in the way they are presented. Before, he wrote as a private individual expressing a private conviction; now he writes as the representative of a group, expounding sectarian dogma. Before, he was a counselor, seeking to persuade; now he is a zealot, determined to destroy. His language throughout the treatise is fierce and fanatical. Catholics he characterizes as "sensualists"; although "members of God's household, they are given to wantonness"; they "find their joy in things of the flesh," for "such things as are of the Spirit, please them not." He indicates a new allegiance and at the same time affirms an old conviction when he declares that "we who are deservedly called the 'spiritual' because of the spiritual charisms we have received . . . admit but one marriage, as we recognize but one God."[1]

There are a number of passages in this treatise which make it clear that Tertullian's extreme views on the illegitimacy of second marriage, expressed so vigorously in earlier writings, had by this time been condemned as heretical,[2] and that his adversaries had appealed to the authority of St. Paul to justify their position and his condemnation.[3] This opposition sufficiently accounts for the polemical tone of the treatise — if it be necessary to account for anything so typical of Tertullian as a controversial attitude. Accordingly, we need not assume that the *De monogamia* was written to answer the charges of some one particular antagonist. Rolffs' conjecture that it was intended as a rebutttal of an anti-Montanist tract of Hippolytus (preserved, supposedly, by Epiphanius, *Haer.* 48. 1-13)[4] cannot be proved and has been generally rejected.[5]

Whatever the occasion of the work, it is quite evident from what has been said above, that it was composed after Tertullian had joined forces with the Montanist party at Carthage.[6] We are thus enabled to date it some time after 212/213 A. D., since it was at this time that he wrote the *De fuga in persecutione*, the treatise which marks his definite break with the Church. It is also reasonably certain that it was composed before the *De ieiunio*,[7] which, in turn, is prior to the *De pudicitia*,[8] apparently Tertullian's last extant work. The *De pudicitia* was written between the years 217 and 222 A. D. Hence, on this evidence, we may say with fair probability that the *De monogamia* was composed between 212 and 222 A. D. Further precision, however, is possible. Tertullian himself tells us that he wrote one hundred and sixty years after St. Paul addressed his first epistle to the Corinthians.[9] Since modern authorities date this epistle in the year 57 A. D., we arrive at 217 A. D. as the most likely date of the *De monogamia*.

The treatise is constructed according to an orderly and easily discernible plan. Tertullian declares in his introduction that Montanism represents a mean between two extremes, heretical repudiation of marriage and Catholic licentiousness in repeating it (1). The doctrine of monogamy, announced authoritatively by the Paraclete, is not an innovation (2-3). It is supported by evidence found in the Old Testament (4-7), the Gospels (8-9), and the Epistles of St. Paul (10-14). To speak of it as harsh and heretical is absurd (15); and the popular arguments advanced to support the practice of second marriage are utterly trivial (16). Finally, Christians ought to be inspired to a love of continence by the example of so many men and women, in and out of the Church, whose lives were models of chastity (17).

Montanism warped Tertullian's judgment and ruined his life, but it did not impair his literary style. In fact, after he threw off the restraining influence of the Church, he began to write with greater passion, with a bolder and more combative eloquence than ever before.[10] The *De monogamia* is a party pamphlet and it follows the party line; yet it is also the work of a brilliant controversialist fighting for a cause very near his own heart. The result is an impressive piece of special pleading, aggressive, abusive, but perfectly sincere. Tertullian is often a sophist, but he is never a hypocrite. He reveals in this treatise all the exasperating self-confidence of the professional reformer and self-appointed custodian of public morals, but his rigorism is joined with a genius for strong language not always found among the puritanical. Perhaps there has never been so slashing a style put at the service of so narrow and illiberal a system. It is one of the great tragedies of the early Church that a man of Tertullian's remarkable talents should have rebelled against the prudent moderation imposed by Catholic orthodoxy, to give himself over with whole-hearted devotion to the propagation of bigotry.[11]

⁄ ⁄ ⁄

The text used for this translation is that of F. Oehler, *Quinti Septimii Florentis Tertulliani quae supersunt omnia* I (Leipzig 1853) 759-87.

Modern translations are:

Kellner, K. A. H., *Tertullians ausgewählte Schriften* 2 (rev. by G. Esser, BKV 24, Kempten-Munich 1916) 473-519.

Thelwall, S., *Tertullian* (repr. in ANF 4, New York 1925) 59-72.

THE USE AND ABUSE OF MARRIAGE

Heretics[1] repudiate marriage; *Sensualists*[2] encourage it.[3] Not *even* once do the former marry, not *only* once the latter. What, then, do you enjoin, O Law of the Creator? Between heretical eunuchs on the one hand and your own extremists[4] on the other, you have as much cause to complain of the libertinism of your household as you have of the puritanism of those who do not belong to you. They injure you as truly who abuse you as do they who use you not. Certainly, their continence deserves no praise, since it is heretical; neither can unrestrained license be defended, since it is rooted in sensuality. The former is blasphemy, the latter, wantonness; the former would do away with the God of marriage, the latter would put Him to the blush.[5]

We, however, who are deservedly called the *Spiritual* because of the spiritual charisms which acknowledgedly are ours, consider that continence is as worthy of veneration as freedom to marry is worthy of respect, since both are according to the will of the Creator. Continence honors the law of marriage, permission to marry tempers it; the former is perfectly free, the latter is subject to regulation; the former is a matter of free choice, the latter is restricted within certain limitations. We admit but one marriage, just as we recognize but one God.

The covenant of marriage is most honorable when it is associated with modesty. But the Sensualists, not receiving the Spirit, take no pleasure in such things as are of the Spirit. Therefore, since such things as are of the Spirit do not please them, they will find their joy in things of the flesh, as being contrary to the Spirit. *For the flesh lusteth against the Spirit,* it is written, *and the Spirit against the flesh.*[6] What does the flesh lust after except more of the flesh? Wherefore, in the beginning it was made a stranger to the Spirit. *My Spirit*, it is written, *shall not remain in these men forever, because they are flesh.*[7]

SECOND MARRIAGE FORBIDDEN BY THE PARACLETE

2. And so they attack the law of monogamy as though it were a heresy; nor have they any cogent reason for rejecting the Paraclete[8] apart from their assumption that He has revealed a completely new way of life, and one indeed, which they find difficult to follow. Therefore, the first point we must take up in our consideration of the subject at hand is whether or not it is possible that the Paraclete has revealed anything at all which is an innovation opposed to Catholic tradition, or which imposes moral obligations upon us inconsistent with the *light burden*[9] referred to by the Lord. The Lord Himself has spoken pertinently on both these subjects. For He says: *I have yet many things to speak to you, but you cannot bear them now; when the Holy Spirit is come, He will introduce you to all truth.*[10] Thus, of course, He sufficiently indicates that the Holy Spirit will reveal such things as may be considered innovations, since they were not revealed before, and burdensome, since it was for this reason that they were not revealed.

But, you object, on the basis of this argument any novelty at all, any oppressive obligation can be called a revelation of the Paraclete, even though it be from the evil spirit. No, certainly not. For the evil spirit would betray himself by the very heterodoxy of his teaching. First of all, he perverts the faith and thus, too, he perverts good morals, because what is first in order must needs be first destroyed; and this means faith, for it is ever the precursor of right conduct. A man's view of God must be heretical before he develops heretical views about His law.

The Paraclete has many things to teach which the Lord deferred until such time as He should come. It is by a predetermined plan that this is done. First He will bear witness to the selfsame Christ in whom we place our faith, and to the whole design of God's creation; and *He will glorify* Him and *bring to mind*[11] the things that He has said. And when thus He is recognized according to the plan which was determined from the beginning, then will He make known the *many things* which have to do with the way of life we are to follow. These things will be authenticated by the integrity of His teaching. They may be new because they are revealed only now, and they may be burdensome because up to now they were not required of us. Nevertheless, their author is the very same Christ who said that He had *yet many other things* which the Paraclete should teach, things which would be found no less a burden by men of our own day than by those who in His day could bear them not.

REVELATION – NOT INNOVATION

3. We shall for the moment leave it to the shameless *infirmity of the flesh*[12] to decide whether or not monogamy is really a burden. In the meantime let us determine whether it be an innovation. Actually, I shall go beyond this and assert that even if the Paraclete had in our day required complete and absolute virginity or continence, so that the hot passion of lust would not have been permitted gratification in even monogamous marriage, not even such legislation could be considered an innovation. For the Lord Himself opened the kingdom of Heaven to eunuchs[13] and He Himself lived

as a eunuch.[14] The Apostle also, following His example, made himself a eunuch and indicated that continence is what he himself prefers.[15]

Yes, you say, but the right to marry still remains. True, it does remain, and with what restrictions it remains we shall see later on. It is already partially abrogated, however, in so far as continence is said to be preferable. *It is good*, he says, *for a man not to touch a woman*. Therefore, it is bad to touch one. For nothing is opposed to the "good" except the "bad."[16] Accordingly, he says that *it remaineth that they also who have wives be as if they had none*.[17] How much more then does it follow that they who *do* not have them, *must* not have them! He adds the reason why he gives this advice when he writes that the unmarried *think on* God, but the married think *how they may please one another* in wedlock.[18]

I might also argue that what is merely permitted is not an absolute good. An absolute good is not a thing that is permitted, but it is legitimate in itself. There is an element of constraint present whenever a permission is granted. So, in the present instance, the one who gives permission to marry does not really wish it. His wish is something quite different, for he says, *I wish you all were even as myself*.[19] And when he points out the *better* course to follow, what else does he intend to say except that he *wishes* us to follow it? Therefore, if he wills one thing and permits another, which he does not will but rather concedes under restraint, he shows that what he unwillingly allows is not an absolute good.

Again, when he says, *It is better to marry than to burn*,[20] what sort of "good" are we to understand that to be which is better than the pain of a punishment, a "good" which cannot be considered as "better" except when it is compared with the worst thing there is? A thing is "good" when it deserves to be called good on its own merits, without any reference, I do not say to evil, but even to another good, so that if it be compared with another good and found inferior, it remains, nevertheless, good in itself. But if we are obliged to call it good when it is placed side by side with something evil, then it is not so much a good as it is a lesser evil. The predication "good" is a forced predication, because the true nature of the thing itself is obscured by the presence of a greater evil.

Take away the term of comparison, so that you do not quote, *It is better to marry " than to burn,"* and I ask whether you would presume to say simply, *It is better to marry,* without indicating precisely what that is with respect to which marriage is better. Therefore, it is no longer really "better"; and since it is not "better," it is not even "good," once the term of comparison is removed which, in making marriage out to be better than something else, forces us to speak of it as "good." It is better to lose one of your eyes than both of them. But if you do not compare these two evils with each other, then it is not really "better" to have just one eye, since this itself is not a good.[21]

What are we to say if all the concessions which the Apostle makes with respect to marriage, are concessions deriving from his own merely human way of looking at things and forced upon him, as we have said, by the consideration that *it is better to marry than to burn?* As a matter of fact, when he turns to another class of persons and writes: *But to them that are married, not I but the Lord giveth commandment,*[22] he indicates that what he said before this was not said on divine authority but according to human prudence. On the other hand, when he directs our attention back again to the subject of continence, he asserts: *For I wish you all to be even as I; and I think that I also have the Spirit of God.*[23] Thus it is his intention to retract, on the authority of the Holy Spirit, any concession which may have been forced from him by necessity.

And John, too, admonishing us that *we ought walk even as the Lord,*[24] is surely admonishing us to walk according to sanctity of the flesh. Indeed, he states this even more clearly: *And every one that hath this hope in Him sanctifieth himself, as He also is holy;*[25] and in another place, *Be ye holy as He also was holy*[26]—that is, in the flesh. He could not have meant "in the spirit," since everybody knows, without being told, that the spirit is chaste;[27] nor need the spirit be exhorted to the practice of chastity, since it is chaste by its very nature. But it is the flesh that is told to be pure, and in Christ this, too, was pure.

Now, if all this, in consideration of the nature of the permission itself and in view of a definitely established preference for continence, abrogates the permission given to marry, then is it impossible that, after apostolic times, the same Holy Spirit[28] should come again in order to introduce a discipline *according to all truth?*[29] It would be in accord with what is most opportune for the times (as it is written in Ecclesiastes, *There is a time for everything*),[30] that in these days the flesh should be pinned down at last, when He dissuades men from marriage, not indirectly as before, but clearly and explicitly. For now more than ever it is true that *the time is short,*[31] considering that about one hundred and sixty years have elapsed since these words were written.[32]

Ought you not to soliloquize somewhat as follows? "This discipline is an ancient one. It was already revealed in our Lord's practice of chastity and in His expressed will on the subject, and later by recommendation and example of His

Apostles. Long ago it was appointed that we should lead lives of chastity such as this. It is no novelty the Paraclete reveals. What He foretold, He now fulfills; what He deferred, He now exacts." Reflecting in this way, you will readily convince yourself, if you understand the will of Christ, that it is all the more reasonable that the Paraclete should preach the doctrine of monogamy, since He could have forbidden marriage altogether, and all the more credible that He should have restricted a concession which it would have been perfectly proper to withdraw completely. Here, also, you ought to recognize the Paraclete as your advocate,[33] since He pleads your weakness as a reason which excuses you from total continence.

THE LAW OF MONOGAMY REVEALED IN GENESIS

4. Let us for the moment omit all reference to the Paraclete (as though He were some private authority of our own) and develop our argument from the books of the ancient Scriptures which all receive.[34] This, then, is what we prove: the law of monogamy is neither new nor foreign to our way of life. Rather it is a law of long standing and one proper to Christianity. Therefore, we ought to acknowledge that the Paraclete has re-established it, and has not promulgated it for the first time.

As regards the antiquity of the law, what form of marriage could be singled out which is older than one found at the very beginning of the human race? God fashioned *one* woman for man, taking only *one* of his ribs, even though he had many. And even before He did this, He said: *It is not good for man to be alone, let us make him a helpmate.*[35] He would have said *helpmates*, if He had intended him to have many wives. This law was also promulgated for future times, since we have the prophetic utterance: *and they will be two in one flesh*;[36] not three or more, for if there were " more," they would be no longer " two."

The law was vested with permanence; and our first parents observed it until the end of their lives, not simply because there were no other women, but because there were none for this very reason that the beginnings of the human race might not be contaminated by bigamy. There could have been other wives, had God so wished. Adam could certainly have taken them from among the great many daughters he had — just as Eve was of his own flesh and bone — if reverence for family ties had permitted this.

After the first crime, murder in the form of fratricide, had come into existence, there was no crime which so fittingly followed as that of bigamy. And here it makes no difference whether a man has two wives simultaneously or successively. The number of individuals involved, whether they come together or separately, is the same.[37] Though God's law was outraged once by Lamech, it thereafter remained inviolate while this race of men endured.[38] There was no second Lamech to imitate the first in marrying two wives. What Scripture does not mention, it denies.[39] There were other and different iniquities which brought on the deluge. Whatever they were, they were punished only once. *Seventy times sevenfold vengeance*[40] was not taken for them, the punishment which bigamy deserved.

Moreover, when the human race was born a second time,[41] once more it has monogamy as its mother. Once more, *two in one flesh* begin to *increase and multiply* — Noe and his wife, along with their sons — and all in monogamy.[42] Even among the animals monogamy can be observed:[43] the very brute beasts were not to be born of adultery. For God said: *Of*

every beast of all flesh, thou shalt bring two into the ark,
that they may live with thee, male and female; there shall be
of fowls according to their kind and of everything that
creepeth on the earth, according to its kind; two of all shall
go in with thee, male and female.[44] On the same principle,
He orders groups of seven pairs to be chosen — one each, male
and female.[45] What more can I say? Not even unclean
birds could enter in company with two females.

ALL THINGS RESTORED IN CHRIST

5. So much for the evidence of antiquity, and the argument for monogamy based on the origin of our race and God's
primeval plan. This, of course, has the force of a law; it is
not merely something to be memorialized.[46] For if we have
a practice that goes back to the beginning, then marriage is
monogamous by law, since we know that Christ wished
things to be as they were in the beginning. For instance,
when the question of divorce came up, He said that *it was*
granted by Moses because of the hardness of their hearts, but
that *from the beginning it was not so.*[47] Thus, indubitably,
He referred to *the beginning* in support of the indissolubility
of marriage. Therefore, *those whom God* from the beginning
has joined together as two in one flesh, let no man put
asunder[48] in our day.

The Apostle, also, writing to the Ephesians, says that God
hath purposed in Himself, in the dispensation of the fullness
of time, to draw back all things in Christ to the head — that is,
to the beginning — *that are in Heaven and on earth in Him.*[49]
In this same way the Lord applied to Himself two Greek
letters, the first and the last, as figures of the beginning and
the end which are united in himself.[50] For just as *Alpha*
continues on until it reaches *Omega* and *Omega* completes

the cycle back again to *Alpha*, so He meant to show us that in Him is found the course of all things from the beginning to the end and from the end back to the beginning, so that every divine dispensation should end in Him through whom it first began, that is, in the Word of God made flesh.[51] Accordingly, it should also end in the selfsame *manner* in which it first began.

And so truly in Christ are all things recalled to their beginning, that the faith has turned away from circumcision back to the integrity of the flesh, as it was from the beginning.[52] So, too, there is liberty now to eat of any kind of food, with abstention from blood alone, as it was in the beginning.[53] There is unity of marriage, as it was in the beginning. There is prohibition of divorce, which was not in the beginning. Finally, the whole man is called once more to Paradise, where he was in the beginning. Why, then, ought not Adam also be restored to Paradise with at least the distinction of monogamy, even though he may not be adorned with the same perfection he had when he was driven forth therefrom?[54]

Therefore, as regards the restoration of what was in the beginning, the faith you follow and the hope you hold both demand that you observe what was from the beginning, according to Him who is the beginning;[55] it began for you with Adam and began again with Noe. Choose from which of these two men you wish to reckon your own origin. In both cases the law of monogamy claims you for itself.

Just as the beginning carries us on to the end, as *Alpha* to *Omega*, and the end returns us once more to the beginning, as *Omega* does to *Alpha*, so our own beginning carries us on to Christ, and the animal ends in the spiritual. For what is first is not spiritual. Rather, the animal is first and only then the spiritual. If this is true, then let us see whether this second origin does not place the self-same obligation upon you as the first. Let us see whether the Second Adam does not present Himself to you in the same condition as the first. And so indeed He does, since the Second Adam, Christ, was wholly disengaged from marriage, even as was the first before his exile.[56] This more perfect Adam, Christ — more perfect because more pure — having come in the flesh to set your infirmity an example, presents Himself to you in the flesh, if you will but receive Him, as a man entirely virginal. If, however, you are not equal to this perfection, He presents Himself to you in the spirit as a model of monogamy: He has one spouse, the Church, as prefigured by Adam and Eve. The Apostle interprets this figure as that *great sacrament . . . in Christ and in the Church.*[57] The analogy [58] of this spiritual monogamy postulates monogamy of the flesh. And so, again, when you return to your origin in Christ, you see that you cannot profess Him without accepting monogamy, without being in the flesh what He is in the spirit; though, of course, you ought also to have been what He was in the flesh.[59]

THE EXAMPLE OF ABRAHAM

6. But let us go on to consider the example of certain other progenitors of ours. For there are those who are not satisfied with Adam and Noe, perhaps not even with Christ. They appeal, for example, to Abraham, even though they are not permitted to call anyone their father but God alone.[60] Well, then, take Abraham for your father; but take Paul also, for he says, *In the Gospel I have begotten you.*[61] Show yourself a true son even of Abraham. Your origin in him is not an indeterminate thing. There is a fixed time in his life when he bears to you the relation of father. For if by reason

of faith we are reckoned sons of Abraham — and we are, as the Apostle teaches in speaking to the Galatians: *You know, therefore, that they who are of faith, the same are the children of Abraham* [62] — then the question arises when it was that Abraham *believed in God and it was reputed to him unto justice.* [63] I rather think it was when he was still living in monogamy, since it was before he was circumcised. [64]

But if afterwards he changed in both of these respects, that is, by the practice of digamy when he lived in concubinage with his handmaid, and by circumcision when he received *the sign of the covenant,* [65] you are then not permitted to recognize him as your father, but only when he believed in God — supposing always that you are his son in the faith and not in the flesh. If you follow Abraham as your father at this later period of his life, that is, when he was a digamist, then accept him also in his circumcision. If you reject him in circumcision, you must also reject him as digamist. You cannot commingle in your own life these mutually exclusive practices of his. He became a digamist when he was circumcised; he was a monogamist when he was uncircumcised. [66] You practice digamy; then receive circumcision. You hold to your uncircumcision; then you are held to monogamy. So true is it that you are a child of Abraham in his life of monogamy and uncircumcision that if you receive circumcision, you are no longer his son, since you are no longer *of faith,* but you will be *of the seal of faith* which was justified in uncircumcision. [67]

You have the Apostle — learn from him, as did the Galatians. [68] If you have involved yourself in digamy, you are not the son of that Abraham who first received his faith while he was living in monogamy. For, though afterwards he is called the *father of many nations,* [69] yet he is the father only of those who were properly reckoned children of his in the faith which he had before he began the practice of digamy. What he did later on does not concern us.[70]

Figures are one thing, forms[71] another. So also types are one thing and laws something quite different. Types no longer exist when they are fulfilled; laws remain always to be observed. Types foretell things that are to come; laws control them. The Apostle shows us what Abraham's digamy typifies when he interprets it as having reference to the two testaments.[72] He also states that our seed is called in Isaac.[73] If you are born of the free woman and so trace your descent from Isaac, then remember that he certainly married only once.

Here, then, I believe, are the men from whom I draw origin. All others I ignore. If I consider the example these others give, then there is David multiplying marriage even by means of murder; there is Solomon, rich even in wives. But you who are told to follow after what is better, have the example of Joseph, a monogamist, and for this reason, I daresay, a better man than his father;[74] you have Moses, who was in closest communion with God;[75] you have Aaron, the High Priest. The second Moses, leader of the second people,[76] was not a digamist. This is he who first bore the name of our Lord and who brought the prototype[77] of the Christian people into the promised land.

THE LESSON OF THE HEBREW LAW

7. Having considered the example given us by the Patriarchs, let us now go on to study the law documented in the Scriptures, so that we may thus examine, in due order, the whole of the sacred canon.[78] There are some who occasionally assert that they are not subject to the Law, the Law

which Christ did not destroy but fulfilled.[79]   Yet on occasion they make it their own, when it suits their purposes to do so.[80] To clarify this subject, we declare that the Law is abrogated in the sense that the burdens which it imposed no longer rest upon us, the burdens, according to the Apostles, which *not even our fathers were able to bear.*[81]   However, such of its precepts as have to do with righteousness not only continue in force but have even been extended, so that our *justice may abound more than that of the Scribes and Pharisees.*[82]   If this holds true of justice, it also holds true of chastity.

Now, it is prescribed in the Law that a man should marry his brother's wife if his brother dies without issue, *in order to raise up seed for his brother.*[83]   This might happen repeatedly, with the same woman involved, as we see in the crafty question put by the Sadducees.[84]   Some imagine from this that in other circumstances also multiple marriage is allowed.   Those who do so ought to understand, first of all, the reason why the command was given.   They would then realize that this reason is no longer valid but is to be reckoned among those parts of the Law which have been abrogated. There was a time when it was necessary for a man to marry the wife of his brother if he died without children: first, because the primeval blessing, *Increase and multiply,* had not yet been fulfilled; second, because the sins of the fathers had to be visited on their sons;[85] third, because eunuchs and the unfruitful were despised.   Accordingly, lest men who died childless because they died prematurely (and not because they were wanting in natural capacity) should be judged accursed, they were provided with offspring of their own blood, vicariously and, as it were, posthumously.

But now that the last days which are upon us have abrogated the precept, *Increase and multiply,* the Apostle introduces a new precept: *It remaineth that they also who have wives be as if they had none, for the time is short.*[86]   And *now no longer the sour grape which the fathers have eaten sets the teeth of the children on edge* since *everyone shall die for his own iniquity.*[87]   Now no longer are eunuchs despised; rather they have merited grace and are invited to enter into the kingdom of Heaven.[88]   Therefore, the law which required a man to marry his brother's wife has been suppressed, and a contrary law has taken its place, that is, the law which forbids him to marry his brother's wife.[89]   And so, as we have said above, a law which has ceased to bind, since the reasons for it are no longer valid, cannot serve as an argument in our day.

Accordingly, a wife is not to remarry if her husband dies, since she will have to marry a brother if she does.   For we are all brethren.[90]   Moreover, if she is going to remarry, she must *marry in the Lord,*[91] that is, she must not marry a pagan, but one of the brethren, since even the Old Law forbade marriage with those of other stock.[92]   And again, in Leviticus we read the warning: *He that marrieth his brother's wife, doth a base and unclean thing; he will die without children.*[93]   Therefore, if a man is prohibited from remarrying in these circumstances, doubtless a woman is also, for she has nobody to marry but a brother.[94]   How the doctrine of the Apostle is consistent with this teaching of the Law — and this he does not reject in its entirety — will be shown when we come to consider his epistle.

In the meantime, let it be noted that arguments based on the Law rather strengthen our position than weaken it.   For example, the Law forbids priests to remarry.[95]   It also requires that the daughter of a priest, *if she be a widow or divorced and if she have no children* must *return to her father's house and eat his bread.*[96] The condition, *if she have no children,* does not mean that if she does have them she ought to marry again, for is there not much less reason for remarriage if she have sons? Rather it means that if she has a son, he, not her father, should support her. Thus, too, her son will fulfill the commandment of God, *Honor thy father and thy mother.*[97]

Jesus, the great High Priest of the Father, clothing us with His own garment — for *those who are baptized in Christ have put on Christ*[98] — has made us priests to God His Father,[99] as John declares. So, too, when He restrained the young man who was hurrying off to bury his father,[100] He did so in order to show us that He has appointed us priests, whom the Law forbade to be present when their parents were buried. Scripture says: *The priest shall not go in at all to any dead person; not even for his father or mother shall he be defiled.*[101] Is this, then, an injunction which we also are obliged to obey? Of course not. For our one Father, God, lives, and so does our Mother, the Church;[102] and neither are we dead who live to God, nor are they dead whom we bury, since they also live in Christ. We are priests in very truth and our vocation is from Christ. So also we are obliged to practice monogamy, since this is according to the ancient law of God which in those days prophesied of us in the priests who were its ministers.

NEW TESTAMENT MODELS

8. And now let us turn to the law under which we ourselves live, that is, to the Gospel. What models do we not see here when we come to examine the text! Lo, on the very threshold, as it were, two Christian priestesses of chastity meet us, Monogamy and Continence: the former, modestly,

in Zachary the priest; the latter, virginally, in John the precursor; the former propitiating God, the latter preaching Christ; the former exemplifying the perfect priest, the latter showing forth one who is more than a prophet [103] — one who not only preached and pointed out the Christ, but who actually baptized Him. For what could be more fitting than that the body of the Lord should receive its initial consecration from one whose flesh was like the flesh which conceived and bore His body? It was a virgin who gave birth to Christ and she was to marry only once, after she brought Him forth. [104] The reason for this was that both types of chastity might be exalted in the birth of Christ, born as He was of a mother who was at once virginal and monogamous.

And at the presentation of the Infant in the temple, who is it that receives Him into his arms? Who first recognized Him in the Spirit? *A man just and God-fearing,* [105] and certainly not a digamist. Otherwise Christ would have been proclaimed more worthily by the aged woman shortly after; for she was a widow who had been married only once; and, in her life of dedication to the temple, she clearly showed what manner of persons should be adherents of the spiritual temple, that is, the Church. Witnesses such as these our Lord had when He was an infant; and in His adult life He had none different. Peter alone, I find, was married, from a reference to his mother-in-law. [106] And I presume that he was married only once since the Church which was built on him [107] would thereafter appoint none but monogamists to places in her hierarchy. Since I do not find that any of the others are referred to as husbands, I am forced to conclude that they were either eunuchs or continent.

Nor may St. Paul be interpreted in such a way as to teach that the Apostles had wives; for among the Greeks one word is used for both "woman" and "wife."[108] This, however, is just a loose usage, since there is a special word for "wives." If the Apostle were discussing the subject of marriage here, as he does later on in a passage where it is more likely he could have illustrated his point by the use of some such example, then he might be correctly considered as saying, *Have we not power to carry about wives, as well as the rest of the Apostles and Cephas?* But when he asks, *Do we not have power to eat and drink?* then he shows that what he is referring to is his non-use of a means of providing for his bodily sustenance. Thus he indicates that they were not wives whom the Apostles brought about with them (for even men who are not married have the right to eat and drink!), but rather women who ministered to their needs in the same way as did the women who accompanied our Lord.[109]

If Christ reproves the Scribes and Pharisees who sat *in the chair of Moses*, yet who did not live the life which they imposed on others,[110] how could He place in His own magisterial office[111] men who would preach chastity but who would fail to practice it, chastity which He always insisted is to be both preached and practiced? In the first place, He shows this by the example of His own life. Then the point is further emphasized when He says that the kingdom of Heaven is for children,[112] associating with them those who, even after marriage, are as children;[113] when He urges us to imitate the simplicity of the dove,[114] a bird which is not only gentle, but which is chaste as well, since one male lives with one female;[115] when He asserts that the Samaritan woman has no husband,[116] and thus makes it clear that pluralism in marriage is adulterous; when, at the revelation of His glory, with so many saints and prophets to choose from, He preferred to appear with Moses and Elias,[117] the one a monogamist, the other a celibate — for Elias was no different from John, who came *in the power and spirit of Elias;* [118] finally, *the man that is a glutton and a winebibber, one who associates with publicans and sinners* at dinners and suppers,[119] is present at only one single wedding,[120] though, obviously, there were many others He might have attended. He chose to be present at marriage no more frequently than He wished it to be celebrated.

CHRIST'S TEACHING ON DIVORCE

9. These arguments might be thought forced and conjectural, if it were not for the teaching of the Lord on the subject of divorce. He prohibits it, even though it had been permitted in earlier days. His reasons are, first, because, like polygamy, *from the beginning it was not so;* [121] second, because *those whom God has joined together man must not put asunder,* [122] lest he act against the Lord's will. He alone may separate husband and wife who has united them in marriage; and He will separate them, not by the harsh method of divorce, which He censures and outlaws, but by the destiny of death. For, *of two sparrows, not one will fall to the ground unless the Father will have it so.* [123] Therefore, if man is not to separate by divorce those whom God has joined together in marriage, it is equally true that man is not to unite in marriage those whom God has separated by death, for he will act against the will of God just as much by joining what has been separated as by separating what has been joined.[124]

Let this suffice on our obligation not to subvert God's will, but rather to revert [125] to His original legislation. There is, moreover, another consideration which is in harmony with this. Rather, it is not "another," but the one which was responsible for the law from the beginning and which moved God to forbid divorce. This is the fact that a man *who puts away his wife, excepting for the cause of adultery, maketh her to commit adultery; and he that shall marry her that is put away by her husband, commits adultery,*[126] as is evident. A divorced woman is not able even to *marry* legitimately, and if she attempts some sort of union which is not marriage, will she not be guilty of the charge of adultery, seeing that adultery is any offense against marriage? It is God's judgment, one quite different from the judgment of men, that all intercourse with a second man, whether in marriage or promiscuously, is adultery — without exception.[127]

Let us see what marriage is in the eyes of God and we shall then see what adultery is as well. A marriage is had when God joins two together in one flesh or, finding them already united, blesses their union.[128] Adultery is committed when these two are separated in any way at all and there is commingling with some other — that is to say, alien — flesh, of which it cannot be said: *This is flesh of my flesh and bone of my bone.*[129] Once this is effected and these words pronounced, it is just as true today as it was in the beginning that they can never be applied in this way again to any other flesh.

It is unreasonable, therefore, to argue that whereas God does not wish a divorced woman to marry a second time if her husband is living, He consents to it if her husband is dead,[130] since if she is not bound to a husband who is dead, no more is she bound to one who is living. You ask: When either divorce or death severs the marriage bond, a wife is free from all obligations, since the bond, the reason for the obligation, is no longer present: to whom, then, would she be under obligation? In the eyes of God there is no difference between a marriage contracted by her after divorce and one contracted after the death of her husband. In neither case does she sin against him, but against herself. *Every sin that a man doth is without the body; but he that committeth adultery sinneth against his own body.*[131]

It is adultery, as I have already pointed out, when a man commingles any flesh with his own, outside that first union in which God joined *two in one flesh* or found them so joined. Therefore, He has abolished divorce, which did not exist *from the beginning,* in order to strengthen what was *from the beginning* — the inseparable union of *two in one flesh.* Lest the necessity of, or the excuse for, a third carnal union arise, He permits divorce for this one reason only, that the offense has already been committed which the prohibition of divorce is intended to prevent.[132] So true is it that divorce was not from the beginning, that among the Romans it is not until the six hundredth year after the foundation of the city that the first instance of such cruel conduct is recorded.[133] They committed adultery, however, although they did not divorce; we, on the contrary, do not even permit remarriage, though we do allow divorce.[134]

THE MARRIAGE BOND STRONGER THAN DEATH

10. I see now, that at this point we shall have to meet an appeal to the authority of the Apostle. In order that we may the more easily arrive at a correct understanding of his doctrine, we must insist very strongly on the particularly serious obligation which a woman has of not remarrying after her husband's death. Let us remember that divorce is either caused by discord or is the cause of it, whereas death is a separation due not to some personal offense, but to the law of

God. Everybody has to die — even people who are not married.

Suppose a woman is divorced because of discord or out of anger or hatred or for causes which lead to these — such as injuries, insults, accusations of one kind or another. Now, if such a woman, though alienated from him in body and soul, is still bound to a man who is her personal enemy (not to speak of him as a husband at all), how much more will a woman who through no fault of her own nor through any fault of her husband, but because it was so ordained in God's law, is widowed, not divorced — be bound to him even after his demise, to whom, even in death, she owes a debt of undivided affection! Since she has not received a bill of divorce from him, she is not separated from him; since she has not written him a bill of divorce,[185] she is still with him. She did not want to lose him — therefore she keeps him. She has as her very own a mind untrammeled, which represents to a person, in imaginary enjoyment, what he does not actually possess.

Suppose that I question the woman herself: "Tell me, sister, did you and your husband part in peace at the hour of his death?" What answer will she give? Will she say, "We were at odds"? In that case she is all the more bound to him, since there is an issue between them which must be settled at the judgment seat of God. She is not separated from a man to whom she is still thus bound. But suppose she says, "We were at peace." In that case she must needs remain at peace with him, since now it is no longer possible for her to divorce him — though, of course, she could not remarry even if it had been possible for her to divorce him.[186]

To be sure, she prays for his soul. She asks that, during the interval, he may find rest and that he may share in the first resurrection.[137] She offers the Sacrifice each year on the anniversary of his falling asleep.[138] If she fails to do this, she has indeed divorced him as far as it lies in her power to do so; and this is all the more wicked because, though she cannot really put him away, she tries her best to do so; and it is all the more shameful in that it is the more shameful to act thus towards one who has not deserved such treatment.

But perhaps we are to follow the doctrine of an Epicurus rather than that of Christ, and suppose that when we die we are annihilated! If we believe in the resurrection of the dead, then we must needs also believe that we will be obliged to give an account of our conduct to one another when we arise together from the dead. In eternity, it is true, *they neither marry nor are married, but shall be like the angels.*[139] Yet, does it follow that because the marriage relationship is not restored, therefore we shall not be bound to spouses who have gone before us in death? On the contrary, we shall be all the more closely bound to them since we are to lead a life superior to that which we have known before. We shall rise to share a spiritual fellowship and in that fellowship we shall be conscious of our own identity as well as the identity of those we love. How shall we sing God's praises world without end if we are not aware of, if we do not remember, the debt we owe Him, if our substance is restored, but we know not who we are?

We who will be with God will also be with one another; for all who are with God are one — even though our reward may be different,[140] even though there are *many mansions* in the house of the same Father.[141] For we all have labored to receive the same wage, the denarius[142] which is life everlasting. And God will no more separate in the life to come those whom He has joined together, than He would have them separated in this lesser life below. Since this is how the matter stands, how will a wife be free to take a second husband, since she belongs entirely to her first, even for all future time? And though my words may seem to be addressed to one sex only, what I say is applicable to persons of both sexes, for there is one law which governs all.[143]

A woman who marries a second time would have one husband in the flesh and another in the spirit. This is adultery—joint knowledge of one woman by two men. If the one is physically separated from her, yet he remains ever present in her heart—there he is still her spouse where, before carnal union is actually effected, one commits adultery by lustful desires[144] and contracts marriage by consenting to its terms.[145] He possesses the very part of her wherein he first became her husband, that is to say, her soul. It is a grievous sin for any other man to find his dwelling there. Her husband, surely, is not excluded from his place just because he no longer traffics in the vulgar commerce of the flesh. Rather, he is a nobler spouse because he is now a purer one.

11. So then, you propose to *marry in the Lord*, as the law and the Apostle require—supposing that you bother about this at all. But how will you dare request the kind of marriage which is not permitted to the ministers from whom you ask it, the bishop who is a monogamist, the presbyters and deacons who are bound by the same solemn obligation,[146] the widows whose way of life you repudiate in your own person?

Our adversaries,[147] it is plain, will give husbands and wives in marriage indiscriminately, as they dole out pieces of bread, for thus they understand the text: *Give to everyone that asketh of you.*[148] They will celebrate your nuptials in a virgin church, the one spouse[149] of the one Christ. You will be

praying for both your husbands, the new and the old alike.
To which of them will you play the adulteress? Take your
choice. I rather think it will be to both. But if you have
sense, you will keep quiet about the one who is dead. To
him let your silence be a bill of divorce, signed and sealed
by your marriage to a stranger. Thus you will win the favor
of your new husband by forgetting your old one. You ought
be especially anxious to please him, since it was for his sake
you preferred not to please God.

ST. PAUL DOES NOT PERMIT SECOND MARRIAGE

Such conduct as this the Sensualists claim the Apostle
either approved or completely overlooked when he wrote:
*A woman is bound as long as her husband liveth; but if her
husband die, she is at liberty. Let her marry whom she will;
only in the Lord.*[150] It is to this passage they appeal in de-
fending the liberty to enter second marriage, indeed, even
multiple marriage, since what ceases to be only once, is
subject to multiplication without end.

The sense in which the Apostle wrote this will become
clear if it is established first of all, that he did not intend it
to have the meaning which the Sensualists adopt. That he
did not intend this meaning is evident when we recall all
there is in his own writings which conflicts with this passage,
when we recall the ideals he proposed and the way of life
which he himself followed.

If he permits second marriage, which was not *from the
beginning*, how can he affirm that *in Christ all things are
brought back to their origin?*[151] If he is willing for us to
marry more than once, how can he defend the proposition
that *our seed is called in Isaac*,[152] a progenitor who was married only once? How can he prescribe that the hierarchy

be monogamous, if laymen, from whose ranks the hierarchy is drawn, are not antecedently bound by the same rule? If he invites men to remarry who have won their freedom by the death of a spouse, how can he call on those who are still actually living together to give up the use of marriage, reminding them as he does, that *the time is short?* If all this is inconsistent with the passage in question, it will be evident, as we have said, that Paul did not intend his words to have the meaning which the Sensualists adopt. Obviously, it is more reasonable to suppose that this one passage has some explanation which is in agreement with all the rest than it is to suppose that the Apostle should seem to contradict himself. We shall be able to discover the correct explanation from an examination of the subject matter itself.

CORRECT EXPLANATION OF HIS TEACHING

What was there in this subject which led Paul to write as he did? There is question here of the inexperience of beginners in a new church, one which was just coming into existence. Naturally, he was nurturing it with milk and not, as yet, with the solid food of more advanced doctrine.[153] Thus it was that in the infant stage of their faith they remained ignorant of what their duty was with respect to the carnal importunities of sex. We can see this illustrated in what he wrote them by way of reply: *Now,* he says, *concerning the things whereof you wrote to me: it is good for a man not to touch a woman. But for fear of fornication let every man have his own wife.*[154] He shows that there were some among them who, being married at the time of their conversion, feared that they were henceforth no longer permitted to make use of marriage because they were incorporated by faith into the pure body of Christ. But he makes this concession *by indulgence, not by commandment;* that is to say, he permits the practice, he does not require it. For he *preferred that all should be even as he himself was.*

Then, in another place, answering a question about divorce, he shows that there were some who had this also in mind, chiefly because they were under the impression that after their conversion to the faith they were not to continue living with a pagan spouse. *Concerning virgins* they had also made inquiry: his *counsel* was (for there was *no commandment of the Lord*) that *it is good for a man so to remain,* that is, to remain as he was at the time of his conversion: *Art thou bound to a wife? Seek not to be loosed. Art thou loosed from a wife? Seek not a wife. But if thou take a wife, thou hast not sinned.* This is because if a man is loosed from his wife before his conversion and then takes another after his conversion, she does not count as his second wife, because she is the first following his conversion — and for us, it is clear, life itself does not begin until we begin to believe. But then he says that in this matter he *spares* them, for otherwise *tribulation of the flesh* would follow them by reason of *the straitness of the times,* which counsels against taking up the burdens of marriage; and that it were better to be *solicitous* about *pleasing the Lord* than a spouse. And so he revokes the permission which he had granted before.

In the very same chapter, then, wherein he teaches that *every man ought to remain in the vocation in which he is called,* he adds the words: *A woman is bound as long as her husband lives; but if he dies, she is free. Let her marry whom she will — only in the Lord.* Here also he shows that the woman in question is one converted to the faith *after* she has been separated from her husband, just as before he had spoken of a husband converted to the faith *after* the death of his wife. The separation is one effected by death, not by divorce, since he would not, in contravention of the precept he had established earlier, permit divorced persons to remarry.

With this understanding of the passage we see why it is that the woman does not sin if she remarries. It is because a man is not considered her second husband who marries her *after* her conversion to the faith. And this is why the Apostle added, *only in the Lord*. He is speaking of a woman who was married to a pagan and converted to the faith after his death. Evidently, he wishes to prevent her from presuming that she is permitted to marry a pagan after her conversion — although the Sensualists are not especially concerned even with this.

Let us understand this clearly: the popular version of our text is at variance with the reading of the authentic Greek original. Two syllables have been changed, either inadvertently or with deliberate intent to deceive: [155] *if her husband will have died.* Here there would be reference to the future and thus the text would seem to be applicable to the case of a woman who loses her husband *after* her conversion. If this were true, then license would have been let loose without any limitation whatsoever, furnishing husbands as often as they were lost, with no respect for marriage remaining at all, not even that which we expect of pagans.

But even suppose the text did have reference to the future. The words, *if her husband will have died*, though indicating the future, would be just as applicable to a woman whose husband died *before* she was converted.[156] Take it either way you wish, as long as you do not destroy the sense of all such passages. The following, for instance, must be in harmony with it: *Wast thou called being a bondman? Care not for it.*[157] *Wast thou called in uncircumcision? Be not cir-*

cumcised. Wast thou called in circumcision? Procure not uncircumcision.[158] It is in this context that we read: *Art thou bound to a wife? Seek not to be loosed. Art thou loosed from a wife? Seek not a wife.*[159] Here it is quite evident that persons are referred to who had been called only recently[160] and were asking for advice regarding the circumstances in which they found themselves at the time of their conversion.[161]

This, then, is our interpretation of the passage. We must examine it to see whether it harmonizes with the time and occasion of writing, with illustrations and arguments used earlier, as well as with assertions and opinions which follow later on, and — most important of all — whether it agrees with the advice of the Apostle and his own personal practice. Obviously, there is nothing to be more sedulously avoided than inconsistency.

THE OBLIGATION OF MONOGAMY NOT RESTRICTED TO CLERICS

12. Now listen to the subtle reasoning of our opponents. They say that the Apostle's permission to remarry is so general that he binds none but clerics to the obligation of monogamy. The fact that he imposes an obligation on *some* proves that he does not impose it on *all*. Well, then, are we to say that an obligation he imposes on all is an obligation from which he exempts bishops alone, seeing that an obligation he imposes on bishops alone is not imposed on all? Or is it rather an obligation for all because it is an obligation also for bishops, and an obligation for bishops because an obligation for all? Whence do we take our bishops and clergy? Is it not from among all of us? And if not all are obliged to monogamy, whence will we have monogamists for the clergy?

Are we to institute some special order of monogamists so that we may choose the clergy from its ranks?

Indeed, whenever we are minded to exalt ourselves with swelling pride at the expense of the clergy, then *we are all one*,[162] then we are all priests, for *He hath made us priests to God and His Father!*[163] But when we are called upon to be the peers of priests in discipline, we lay aside our fillets — and pair off![164]

The question under consideration concerned the qualities required in men who were to receive orders in the Church. It was necessary, then, that the law which was meant for all should be shown forth in the persons of those who stand in the forefront of the Church so that in this way the binding force of the edict would, in some measure, be impressed upon all and so that the members of the laity might understand the better their own obligation to follow a way of life which conditions men for leadership; and the men in Orders were themselves not to beguile themselves into the belief that they were permitted to do as they pleased, as though by some special privilege of their position. The Holy Spirit saw that in the future some would say: " All things are permitted to bishops! " And, in fact, your bishop of Uthina is a case in point: he did not scruple to violate even the edict of Scantinius![165] And how many digamists are there who rule in your churches,[166] obviously insulting the Apostle, or at least unembarrassed, even as his words on this subject are read out while they are presiding!

Come now, you who think that the law of monogamy is binding on bishops alone, cease practicing the rest of those virtues[167] which, along with monogamy, are written down as proper to the episcopal order. Be not *blameless, sober, of good behavior, orderly, hospitable, ready to be taught*; but rather

69313

be *given to wine, quick to strike, ready to pick a quarrel, a lover of money, negligent of domestic discipline, careless in governing your children, indifferent to the good testimony of them who are without.*[168] For if bishops have their own peculiar law of monogamy, then these other qualities also which must go along with monogamy, have been set down for bishops only. Accordingly, laics, since they are not bound by the law of monogamy, are not bound by the other virtues either. In this way, my dear Sensualist, you succeed in escaping, if this is what you wish, the obligations of the whole moral code. But be consistent. Lay it down that precepts given to some are not binding on all; or, if you will have it that monogamy is prescribed for bishops only, but that the rest of the virtues are to be practiced by all members of the community, would you then say that only they should be called Christians who are obliged to follow the Christian code in its entirety?

FURTHER EXAMINATION OF THE APOSTLE'S TEACHING

13. Another objection they urge is this: writing to Timothy, Paul *wishes young women to marry, to bear children, to be mothers of families.*[169] He is directing his words to those women only whom he reproaches earlier, that is, *young widows* who were converted to the faith *after* the death of their husbands. When they have been followed by suitors for a while — *when they have wantonly turned away from Christ, they wish to marry, having damnation because they have made void their first faith,*[170] the faith, that is, to which they were converted in their widowhood, the faith which they professed and then did not retain. It is for this reason that he *wishes* them to marry; he wishes to keep them from

making void the first faith of their widowhood. He does not wish women to marry whenever, in their widowed state, being tempted or even *grown wanton*, they lose their desire to persevere.

We also read what Paul writes to the Romans: *The woman that hath a husband, whilst her husband liveth is bound to him. But if he be dead, she is loosed from the law of her husband. Therefore, whilst her husband liveth, she shall be called an adulteress if she be with another man: but if her husband be dead, she is delivered from the law; so that she is not an adulteress if she be given to another man.*[171] But now read the rest of the passage, and the meaning which you find so agreeable is seen to be impossible. He says: *Therefore, my brethren, be ye also made dead to the law by the body of Christ, that you may belong to another, to Him, namely, who is risen again from the dead, that we may bring forth fruit to God. For when we were in the flesh, the passions of sins which were caused by the law (did work) in our members to bring forth fruit unto death. But now we are loosed from the law, being dead to that in which we were bound, so that we should serve God in newness of spirit and not in the oldness of the letter.*[172] Now, if the Apostle commands that we *be made dead to the law by the body of Christ*, which is the Church — and the Church abides *in newness of spirit, not in the oldness of the letter*, which is the law — then he nullifies for you the law which permits a wife to marry again after the death of her husband. He subjects you to a law which is just the opposite, commanding you *not* to marry, if your husband dies.[173] It is true that you would not be considered an adulteress in remarrying after your husband's death, if you were still bound to live according to the Law. It is just as true, now that you are placed in different circumstances, that the Apostle condemns you as an adulteress if you marry another after your husband dies. For now you are *made dead to the law* and, therefore, no longer free to do this, since you are no longer under the Law which permitted you to do so.

14. Even if the Apostle had granted a general permission that converts might remarry who lost husband or wife after conversion to the faith, yet this would have been done in accordance with a policy he followed in other situations when the circumstances of the times led him to act against his established norms. Thus he circumcised Timothy because of false, supposititious brethren.[174] On another occasion, because of the close watch the Jews kept on his conduct, he brought into the Temple certain men with shaven heads.[175] Yet this is the same Paul who castigates the Galatians when they desire to live according to the Law.[176] Such concessions were called for by the exigencies of each case, in order that he might be *all things to all men, that he might save all,*[177] *being in labor until Christ be formed in them.*[178] These little ones of the faith he cherished as a nurse and on occasion taught in a spirit of indulgence, and not as one imposing strict obligations. For it is one thing to concede, another to command. Thus, as a temporary concession, he allows second marriage because of the *infirmity of the flesh*, just as Moses had permitted divorce because of the *hardness of men's hearts.*[179]

Here, then, is an explanation of the full sense of the Apostle's words. If Christ abrogated a law of Moses because *from the beginning it was not so* and yet is not, on this account, to be reputed as having come in some power other than that of Moses,[180] why could not the Paraclete, too, have revoked an indulgence which Paul allowed, seeing that second marriage was not *from the beginning* any more than divorce? Why could He not do this—provided only that His revelation be worthy of God and Christ—without becoming suspect, as though He were some alien Spirit? If it was proper that God and Christ should, in the fullness of time, chasten men's *hardness of heart*, why is it not even more fitting that God and Christ could reject the plea of *infirmity of the flesh*, now that *the time is short?* If justice demands that marriage be undivided, then, certainly, honor requires that it be not repeated. Both are reckoned, even in the judgment of the world, as properties which right order demands—the one in the name of peace, the other, of decency. *Hardness of heart* prevailed until the coming of Christ; it should be enough that *infirmity of the flesh* prevailed until the coming of the Paraclete. The new law abrogated divorce, which was a definite abuse that had to be ended; the new prophecy outlaws second marriage, which is just as truly the dissolution of a prior marriage.

But *hardness of heart* yielded to Christ more easily than does *infirmity of the flesh*. The latter appeals with greater pertinacity to Paul than the former does to Moses—if that can be called an appeal which snatches at Paul's concessions and refuses his demands, which seeks to evade the force of his dearest convictions and to frustrate his prevailing intentions, which does not suffer us to honor the Apostle by carrying out in our lives what he himself prefers.

How long will this shameless *infirmity* continue to oppose[181] the better things? It had its day before the working of the Paraclete; it was until His coming that the Lord put off the *things they could not yet bear.*[182] But there is no one who *cannot bear them now*, for He is at hand who gives us the ability to do so. How long will we continue to plead our flesh in excuse, just because the Lord has said: *the flesh is weak?* [183] Notice that first He said: *The spirit is willing,* in order that the spirit might overcome the flesh and that weakness might give way to strength. He also said: *He that can take it, let him take it,* [184] implying that he who cannot take it should go his way. This is what that rich man did who refused to follow the command to give his substance to the poor. He went his way, and the Lord abandoned him to the decision which he made. [185] Nor should Christ be charged with harshness when it is really a man's own free will which is at fault. [186] *Behold,* Scripture says, *I have placed before thee . . . good and . . . evil.* [187] Choose the good. But if you are unable to do this because you do not *wish* to do it—and in proposing both good and evil to your choice He shows that you are able to choose the good if you wish—then you must depart from Him whose will you do not obey.

THE DOCTRINE OF MONOGAMY NEITHER HARSH NOR HERETICAL

15. Why, then, are we considered hardhearted if we separate ourselves from persons who refuse to do the will of God? What heresy is there in judging second marriage as illicit, the next thing to adultery? [188] What is adultery, after all, but illicit marriage? The Apostle censures those who *forbid marriage* absolutely as well as those who forbid *the use of meats, which God hath created.* [189] Now, we no more outlaw marriage when we prohibit its repetition than we condemn food when we fast frequently. Prohibition is one thing, moderation is another. It is one thing to make a law forbidding all marriage and something quite different to limit marriage.

A plain question may be put to those who accuse us of

harshness or who see heresy in the position we here adopt. If they coddle *infirmity of the flesh* to such an extent that they imagine it is to be pampered by frequent marriage, why do they not pamper and coddle it with forgiveness in other circumstances — when instruments of torture have forced it to apostatize? Certainly, infirmity which succumbs in battle [190] is more easily excused than that which succumbs in the boudoir; that which gives way on the rack than that which gives way on the bridal bed; which yields to cruelty rather than concupiscence; which is conquered, groaning with pain, than that which is conquered, burning with lust. Yet because of infirmity in the first case they excommunicate a person, since he did not *persevere to the end*; [191] while a weakling of the other type is received to communion, just as though he had *persevered to the end*. Call to mind precisely why it was that each failed to *persevere to the end*, and you will find more reason to justify the man who could not endure cruelty than the one who could not endure chastity. Yet *infirmity of the flesh* does not excuse a man whose lapse is the result of torture; far less does it excuse one whose lapse is the result of lust. [192]

SOPHISMS OF THE SENSUALISTS

16. I have to laugh when they come with the counter-argument of the *infirmity of the flesh*; this supposed infirmity should rather be called consummate strength. To marry a second time is a thing which calls for real virility! To rise from the easy relaxation of continence and fulfill the functions of sex — this is to prove oneself a man indeed! Weakness such as this is strong enough for a third, fourth, perhaps even a seventh marriage, since its strength increases as its weakness grows, until at length it can no longer claim the

Apostle as its authority, but a man like Hermogenes, who marries more women than he paints.[193] This man is immersed in matter and since he imagines that the soul itself is material,[194] he is all the more lacking in the Spirit of God. He is no longer even a Psychic[195] because his *psyche* is not derived from the divine *afflatus*.

What are we to say if someone alleges poverty as an excuse and acknowledges that in remarrying he has undoubtedly prostituted his body, but asserts that he has done so in order to sustain his life — forgetting that we are not to be *solicitous for food and raiment?*[196] He has God to turn to, God who cares for even the ravens, and cultivates even the flowers. But suppose he pleads the loneliness of his life at home as an excuse? As though one woman could be company for a man who is on the point of flight![197] Of course, he may take one of the widows to live with him. He may have not just one wife such as this but even a great many.[198] But what if a man, with thoughts like the eyes of Lot's wife,[199] is anxious about posterity and desires a second marriage because he has no children by his first? To think that a Christian, one who is disinherited by all the world, should be hunting around for heirs! He has brethren. He has the Church, his Mother. The case is different, however, if they suppose that the forum of Christ follows the Julian Laws, and if they imagine that unmarried persons and persons without children are prohibited, by a divine decree, from inheriting the full share of their patrimony.[200]

Let all such persons as these keep right on marrying up to the end of the world, so that on the day when all flesh will be confounded they may be overtaken by that fated and final catastrophe, as were Sodom and Gomorrha and those who lived at the time of the deluge. They must add to the text,

Let us eat and drink, a third exhortation — "Let us get married also," *for tomorrow we shall die.*[201] They fail to reflect that the *woe* of *those that are with child and that give suck*[202] will be far more serious and far more bitter when the whole world is stricken than it was when one little corner of Judea was destroyed. Let them then harvest the fruit of their repeated nuptials — right seasonable fruits they are for the latter days — swollen breasts and nauseating wombs and whimpering infants. Let them provide for Antichrist, so that his savage cruelty may wanton all the more. He will give them midwives — the public executioners![203]

PAGAN CHASTITY A JUDGMENT ON THE FLESH

17. That everlasting *infirmity of the flesh!* A pretty plea of privilege this will be before the judgment seat of Christ! But it will no longer be the monogamous Isaac, our father, who will pass on it; nor John,[204] a celibate of Christ; nor Judith, the daughter of Merari;[205] nor the many other saints who have given us example. Pagans are appointed as our judges.[206] A queen of Carthage will rise up and pass sentence on the followers of Christ. As a fugitive in an alien land and on the point of founding a mighty city, she ought naturally to have been anxious to wed a king; yet, lest she be guilty of bigamy, she preferred *to burn* rather than *to marry.* With her will be seated a Roman matron. Because she knew a man who was not her husband, though it was by violence forced on her at night, she cleansed the defilement of her flesh by shedding her own blood, willing to make compensation for the loss of her chastity at the cost of her life. There have been women, too, who preferred to die for their husbands' sake rather than remarry after they were gone.[207]

The false gods, as everybody knows, have widows and

monogamists to serve them. None but a woman married only once may crown *Fortuna Muliebris*.[208] The same is true of *Mater Matuta*.[209] The *Pontifex Maximus* and the wife of the *Flamen* are monogamists.[210] The priestesses of Ceres are women who, during their husbands' lifetime and with their husbands' consent, amicably dissolve their marriage and embrace the widow's state. Then there are others who will judge us on our practice of perfect continence: the Vestal Virgins and the virgins who attend the Achaean Juno and the Scythian Diana[211] and the Pythian Apollo.[212] Even the priests who are dedicated to the service of that Egyptian bull will, by their practice of celibacy, pass sentence on the *infirmity* of Christians.

EPILOGUE

Blush, thou flesh, flesh that hast *put on Christ*.[213] It should be enough for you to marry only once. This is what your origin demands of you, this is what the end recalls you to. Return to the example of the first Adam, at least, if you are unable to imitate the Second. Once only did he taste of the tree; once only felt he concupiscence; once only covered up his nakedness; once only blushed before God and hid himself for shame; once only was he driven forth, an exile, from the Paradise of chastity[214] and, after that, he married only once. If you were *in him*[215] then, you have a norm for your conduct now; if you follow Christ, you ought to be better still. Show us a third Adam — one who is a digamist; then only may you adopt a manner of life such as the other two do not allow.

NOTES

LIST OF ABBREVIATIONS

AC   F. J. Dölger, Antike und Christentum
ACW   Ancient Christian Writers
ANF   Ante-Nicene Fathers
BKV   Bibliothek der Kirchenväter, ed. by O. Bardenhewer, T. Schermann, C. Weyman
CE   Catholic Encyclopedia
CSEL   Corpus scriptorum ecclesiasticorum latinorum
DACL   Dictionnaire d'archéologie chrétienne et de liturgie
DCA   Dictionary of Christian Antiquities
DTC   Dictionnaire de théologie catholique
ES   Enchiridion symbolorum, 21st ed., ed. by H. Denziger, C. Bannwart, J. B. Umberg
LCL   Loeb Classical Library
LF   A Library of Fathers of the Holy Catholic Church
LTK   Lexikon für Theologie und Kirche
Mansi   Sacrorum conciliorum nova et amplissima collectio
ML   P. J. Migne, Patrologia latina
OCD   Oxford Classical Dictionary
RAC   Reallexikon für Antike und Christentum
RE   Realenzyklopädie der classischen Altertumswissenschaft
SCA   Studies in Christian Antiquity
SPCK   Society for Promoting Christian Knowledge
TLL   Thesaurus linguae latinae
TWNT   Theologisches Wörterbuch zum Neuen Testament

TO HIS WIFE

INTRODUCTION

[1] See, for example, J. Tixeront, *History of Dogmas* (tr. from the 5th French ed. by H. L. B., St. Louis 1910) 1. 323.

[2] *Ad ux.* 1. 7. For a useful synopsis of Tertullian's views on marriage and remarriage, cf. H. Preisker, *Christentum und Ehe in den ersten drei Jahrhunderten* (Berlin 1927) 187-200.

[3] Cf. Rom. 7. 2 f.; 1 Cor. 7. 8 f., 39 f.; 1 Tim. 5. 14.

⁴ The Eastern Church judged second marriage more severely than did the Church in the West. Athenagoras (*Suppl.* 33), writing on the Christian ideal of chastity in marriage, declares that the man who takes a second wife after the death of his first is a ' cloaked adulterer.' Clement of Alexandria (*Strom.* 3. 12. 82. 4) considers that such unions are a mark of imperfection, while Origen (*Hom. in Luc.* 17) says that digamists will be saved in the name of Christ, but will not be among those who are crowned by Him. The earliest statement in the Western Church is that of the *Pastor Hermae* (*mand.* 4. 4), to the effect that one who remarries does not sin ' but, if he dwells by himself, he acquires great honor to himself with the Lord.' It is to this doctrine of the *Pastor Hermae* that Tertullian alludes when, in the Montanist treatise *De pudicitia* (10), he speaks of the scripture of the Shepherd, which is the only one that favors adulterers and which has not found place in the divine canon.' For a comparative study of the views on this subject which prevailed in the East and West, cf. G. H. Joyce, *Christian Marriage* (2nd ed. London 1948) 584-600; on the teaching of Athenagoras, see K. v. Preysing, ' Ehezweck und zweite Ehe bei Athenagoras,' *Theol. Quartalschrift* 110 (1929) 115 ff. The early history of the whole question is well summarized by F. Meyrick, ' Marriage,' DCA 2. 1103 f.; see also A. Knecht, *Handbuch des katholischen Eherechts* (Freiburg i. Br. 1928) 750-53. The most detailed study of successive polygamy, from the viewpoint of dogmatic theology, is still that of J. Perrone, *De matrimonio Christiano* (Rome 1858) 3. 74-111; for a less complete, though more modern treatment, see C. Boyer, *Synopsis praelectionum de sacramento matrimonii* (Rome 1947) 58-60. Official pronouncements of the Church on the subject may be found in ES 55, 424, 465, 541. It is the Church's teaching here that even *tertia et ulteriora matrimonia* may be contracted without sin. This reflects the doctrine of St. Jerome and St. Augustine. St. Jerome writes (*Epist.* 49. 8): ' *Non damno bigamos et trigamos et, si dici potest, octogamos*'; and St. Augustine (*De bono vid.* 12): ' *De tertiis et quartis et de ultra pluribus nuptiis solent homines movere quaestionem. Unde et breviter respondeam: nec ullas nuptias audeo damnare, nec eis verecundiam numerositatis auferre.*' — On the history of the special discipline for clerics, cf. J. M. Ludlow, ' Digamy,' DCA 1. 552 f.; and below, n. 65.

⁵ *De bono vid.* 4. 6; *De haer. ad Quodvultdeum* 86. In the latter passage Tertullian is said to have become a heretic *quia transiens ad*

Cataphrygas . . . coepit etiam secundas nuptias contra apostolicam doctrinam tamquam stupra damnare.

[6] *Comm. in Epist. ad Titum* 1. 6.

[7] This is in disaccord with the opinion of Vincent of Lerins who, in a famous description of Tertullian's ability as a writer, says (*Comm.* 24): *Iam porro orationis suae laudes quis exsequi valeat, quae tanta nescio qua rationum necessitate conferta est, ut ad consensum sui, quos suadere non potuerit, impellat: cuius quot paene verba, tot sententiae sunt; quot sensus, tot victoriae?*

[8] J. Tixeront, *A Handbook of Patrology* (tr. from the 4th French ed. by S. A. Raemers, St. Louis 1944) 110. His judgment is that Tertullian is an 'implacable logician,' though he 'has the defects of his qualities' and 'his logic runs to paradox.' See also O. Bardenhewer, *Geschichte der altkirchlichen Literatur* 2 (2nd ed. Freiburg i. Br. 1914) 383 f.; P. de Labriolle, *History and Literature of Christianity from Tertullian to Boethius* (tr. from the French by H. Wilson, London-New York 1924) 94-96.

[9] On the problem of mixed marriages in the ancient Church see J. Köhne, *Die Ehen zwischen Christen und Heiden in den ersten christlichen Jahrhunderten* (Paderborn 1931); the same, 'Über die Mischehen in den ersten christlichen Zeiten,' *Theol. und Glaube* 23 (1931) 333-50.

[10] The statement is made by J. Fessler, *Institutiones Patrologiae* (ed. B. Jungmann, Innsbruck 1890) 1. 272.

[11] Tertullian's style has not always been as highly esteemed by Latinists as it is today. A celebrated German philologist of the 18th century, David Ruhnken, states flatly: '*Tertullianum latinitatis certe pessimum auctorem esse aio et confirmo*' (quoted by E. F. Leopold, *Zeitsch. f. hist. Theol.* 8 [1838] 33).

[12] T. R. Glover, *Tertullian: Apologia, De Spectaculis* (LCL, London 1931) xxvi. J. H. Waszink believes that with Tertullian, as with Aristotle, paraphrases of the text 'serve the purpose of correct understanding better than literal translations'; cf. *Quinti Septimi Florentis Tertulliani: De anima* (Amsterdam 1947) ix. It is the opinion of so competent a critic as A. Souter that Tertullian is the most difficult of all Latin prose writers; cf. *Tertullian: Concerning Prayer and Baptism* (SPCK, London 1919) xi.

[13] A. Harnack, *Die Chronologie der altchristlichen Litteratur bis Eusebius* 2 (Leipzig 1904) 273.

[14] Cf. St. Jerome, *De viris illustribus* 53.

[15] *Ibid.*

¹⁶ See the review of this volume by B. Capelle, in the *Bulletin de théologie ancienne et médiévale* 4, suppl. bibl. (1943) [8 f.].

TEXT

¹ *Praelegare* is a technical legal expression used to indicate that a bequest is made before an inheritance is finally divided. The text of this sentence has caused editors considerable difficulty; the present translation is based on Kroymann's reading.

² Judged by modern standards the involved rhetoric of this introductory paragraph may seem artificial and forced. Its legal flavoring is typical of Tertullian, whose early training in jurisprudence gave him a familiarity with, and fondness for, this kind of language. The phrase 'receive in its entirety' is an allusion to the *solidi capacitas* of Roman testamentary law. Under Augustus an unmarried person (*coelebs*) was not permitted to inherit at all; childless couples (*orbi*) were allowed to receive only the half of their inheritance; parents of three or more children were granted numerous privileges and benefits. See W. W. Buckland, *A Textbook of Roman Law from Augustus to Justinian* (2nd ed. Cambridge 1932) 292, for the restrictions imposed by the *Lex Iulia* and the *Lex Papia*. — Tertullian speaks of the advice he gives his wife as a *fideicommissum*, that is, a bequest which is delivered in trust (*precative*) rather than by command (*ex rigore iuris civilis*). Cf. *Digests* 30-32 and Buckland, *op. cit.* 353-60. — *Demonstratio*, in the law of procedure, means a clear declaration of purpose or intent: see *Digests* 35. 1 and Buckland, *op. cit.* 649. — For the doxology, see Jude 25; Apoc. 5. 13.

³ Cf. Matt. 22. 23-30; Mark 12. 18-26; Luke 20. 27-36.

⁴ Our Lord's answer shows that the *contretemps* envisaged by the Sadducees will not arise, since there is no such thing as posthumous jealousy. Therefore it is not out of consideration for her deceased husband that a wife should avoid remarriage. The question to be investigated is whether it is to the advantage of the widow herself to remain single.

⁵ The words are *replendo orbi*. Cf. Gen. 1. 28. Tertullian is at one with the constant tradition of the Church in teaching that the primary purpose of marriage is the procreation of children.

⁶ *Instruendo saeculo*. *Saeculum* has the root meaning of ' race,' ' breed,' ' generation.' Should this sense seem unwarranted here, the words may be translated ' to furnish and adorn the world,' with a reference to Gen. 2. 1.

[7] See Gen. 2. 21 f. Tertullian appears to be pleased with this conceit. He expands it in *De exhort. cast.* 5 and repeats the idea in *De monog.* 4. It is imitated by St. Jerome, *Adv. Iovin.* 1. 14 and *Epist.* 123 (*Ad Geruchiam de monogamia*) 11. Innocent III uses it in his letter *Gaudemus in Domino*, forbidding the practice of polygamy to converts from paganism. Cf. ES 408.

[8] *Fas fuit*, a stronger expression than many theologians and exegetes use today in speaking of the polygamy of the Patriarchs.

[9] The meaning of the sentence remains obscure, but the implication seems to be that the passages are to be taken allegorically because they have to do with the old dispensation as a type of the new. Since they are to be understood in a figurative or allegorical sense, we should not be surprised if there is some difficulty in their interpretation. Tertullian's theory of Biblical exegesis is essentially sound. He insists that the interpretation of Scripture belongs to the Church (cf. *De praescr. haer.* 37) and deprecates the abuse of the allegorical method. Unfortunately, in practice, especially during his Montanist period, he ignores many of his own principles. See A. d'Alès, *La théologie de Tertullien* (3rd ed. Paris 1905) 242-54.

[10] Cf. Rom. 5. 20.

[11] The idea of spiritual circumcision, or circumcision of the heart, was known also to the Old Testament: cf. Lev. 26. 41; Deut. 10. 16; Jer. 44. See also the claim by the allegorizing author of the Epistle of Barnabas (9. 4) that such circumcision had been commanded in the Old Law, but that the Jews, 'deluded by a bad angel,' misinterpreted this as circumcision to be practiced in the flesh.

[12] *Passivus*, in the sense of 'widespread,' 'general' (*pando, passim*), is frequent in Tertullian: cf. *Apol.* 9; *De pall.* 3, 4; *De pud.* 2; also Oehler's note, 1. 437.

[13] Cf. 1 Cor. 10. 11, 2 Tim. 3. 1. The proximity of the parousia was a fundamental tenet of Montanism, and Tertullian seems to have been excessively sympathetic to the belief well before his actual defection from the Church. The connection between this conviction and his exaggerated asceticism is obvious. For a full discussion of this point see P. de Labriolle, *La crise montaniste* (Paris 1913) 107 ff.

[14] S. Thelwall, following Oehler, translates: 'Therefore, by means of the wide license of those days, materials for subsequent emendations were furnished beforehand, of which materials the Lord by His gospel, and then the Apostle in the last days of the (Jewish) age, either cut off the redundancies or regulated the disorders.'

[15] The reference is to the Marcionites. In *Adv. Marc.* 1. 29 Ter-

tullian says that these heretics baptized none but virgins, widows, celibates, and women who had purchased baptism by separating from their husbands.

[16] Cf. Gen. 2. 24; Matt. 19. 5 f.

[17] The *Agobardinus* has *matrimonii computatione*, the reading adopted here. Kroymann prefers *compactione*.

[18] 1 Cor. 7. 1 f. and 26.

[19] *Depretiare* is a post-Augustan legal term. Cf. Oehler 1. 279.

[20] See 1 Cor. 7. 9. The argument here drawn from the text is often repeated: cf. *De pud.* 1, 16; *De exhort. cast.* 3; *De monog.* 3. St. Jerome, whom Tertullian strongly influenced, has it in his treatise *Adv. Iovin.* 1. 7, 9. He writes that 'better' has no reference to an absolute good but is always compared to 'the worse.' It is as though the Apostle were to illustrate the point by saying that 'it is better to have one eye than none.'

[21] Cf. Matt. 10. 23.

[22] The sense of this paragraph is very difficult to get at and many reconstructions have been attempted. The translation given here owes most to Rigault's reading: cf. N. Rigaltius, *Q. S. F. Tertulliani Opera* (2nd ed. Paris 1675) 162 f. Fear to use the permission to flee shows a recognition of something unworthy in the act of flight, a recognition that it is better, because more consistent with Christian virtue, not to flee in the face of persecution, even though this is permitted. Similarly, Tertullian argues, it is better for the Christian not to marry, even though he is allowed to do so. The whole passage illustrates the justice of Professor Waszink's observation that the difficulty in Tertullian is not his idiom but the sequence of his thought: *op. cit.* ix. — Flight in times of persecution was a problem apparently solved by the Lord Himself (cf. Matt. 10. 17-23), yet the centuries of persecution brought much discussion of the question. In his *De fuga in persecutione* the Montanist Tertullian categorically condemns such flight as apostasy. Cyprian and Athanasius found it necessary to defend their action in evading the persecutor's dragnet. St. Augustine took up the problem when the Vandals invaded Africa. Cf. E. Jolyon, *La fuite de la persécution pendant les trois premiers siècles du christianisme* (Lyon 1903); T. Ortolan, 'Fuite pendant la persécution,' *DTC* 6. 1 (1920) 951-64; for Tertullian, d'Alès, *op. cit.* 454-60.

[23] Compare the use of *praelatio* here with a parallel passage in *Apol.* 13: *Praelatio alterius sine alterius contumelia non potest procedere, quia nec electio sine reprobatione.*

[24] Phil. 3. 13.

[25] 1 Cor. 12. 31. Tertullian has *meliorum donativorum sectatores*, the Vulgate *aemulamini autem charismata meliora*. It is impossible to say with certainty what version or versions of the Scriptures Tertullian used. De Labriolle (*op. cit.* 45) believes that he habitually translates his quotations from the original Greek, but that he also had various Latin versions before his eyes. Cf. the same author's argument in the *Bulletin d'ancienne littérature et d'archéologie chrétienne* 4 (1914) 210-13; also H. Rönsch, *Das Neue Testament Tertullians* (Leipzig 1871), and H. von Soden, *Der lateinische Paulustext bei Marcion und Tertullian* (Festgabe A. Jülicher, Tübingen 1927) 229-81. For the literature on the ancient Latin versions of the Scriptures, see P. A. Vaccari, *Institutiones Biblicae* I (Rome 1933) 271. P. Monceaux studies the question of these versions with special reference to Africa in his *Histoire littéraire de l'Afrique chrétienne* I (Paris 1901) 97-173.

[26] 1 Cor. 7. 35.

[27] *Ibid.* 7. 34.

[28] Cf. *ibid.* 7. 40.

[29] Matt. 26. 41.

[30] The Greek (*ibid.*) is πρόθυμον. The Vulgate has *promptus*; Tertullian, *firmus*. Elsewhere he regularly reads *promptus*: *Ad mart.* 4; *De monog.* 14; *De pat.* 13.

[31] *Sensus* often means 'sentence' in post-Augustan Latin.

[32] *Servi Dei* is a standing expression for 'Christians,' distinguishing them from the *diaboli servi*, 'servants of the devil' — 'pagans.' Catechumens were numbered among the *servi Dei*, though to distinguish the baptized Christian from the catechumen, the former was called *perfectus servus Dei*. Further, lay persons were termed *servi minoris loci*, the clergy (deacons, presbyters, bishops), *servi maioris loci*. Cf. S. W. J. Teeuwen, *Sprachlicher Bedeutungswandel bei Tertullian* (Stud. z. Gesch. u. Kultur d. Albert. 14. 1, Paderborn 1926) 126-28.

[33] These are part of the *pompa diaboli* (cf. e. g. Tertullian, *De cor.* 13) which we renounce (*abrenuntiatio*) in baptism. Cf. J. H. Waszink, 'Pompa diaboli,' *Vigiliae Christ.* 1 (1947) 13-41.

[34] The expression is *officia aetatis*. Below (2. 3), Tertullian writes of the *officia sexus*. The word *debitum* in 1 Cor. 7. 3 has a connotation somewhat similar to that of *officia* in these passages. *Aetas* here may mean 'mature life' or 'the prime of life' or, simply, the age at which they have actually arrived, therefore 'proper to their age of life.' St. Paul, 2 Tim. 5. 11 and 14, implies that it is youth

which makes continence difficult for widows, and Tertullian may mean that it is the plea of youth which is used to justify remarriage. *Aetas* certainly means 'youth' in the following sentence.

[35] Phil. 3. 19.

[36] The words are '. . . *dignationem velut munera maritalia.*' On the *donatio propter nuptias* of husband to wife, see C. P. Sherman, *Roman Law in the Modern World* (New York 1937) 2. 67; also the extensive literature on this subject listed by Buckland, *op. cit.* iii.

[37] *Insufficientia* is late Latin. Its meaning here is graphically illustrated by a passage in one of St. Jerome's letters, *Epist.* 54 (*Ad Furiam*) 15. He writes: 'Young widows are wont to say: "My little estate is wasting every day, the property I have inherited is being scattered, my footman has spoken insultingly to me, my maid pays no attention to my orders. Who will appear for me in court? Who will be responsible for my land tax? Who will educate my little children and bring up my house-slaves?"' Tertullian says such arguments are suggested by concupiscence of the world, but Jerome believes that they are pretexts suggested by concupiscence of the flesh. See *Select Letters of St. Jerome* (tr. by F. A. Wright, LCL, London 1933) 255.

[38] *Alienis opibus incubare*: compare Virgil's *incubare auro* (*Georg.* 2. 507) and *incubare divitiis* (*Aen.* 6. 610); also Ambrose's *thesauro suo die ac nocte incubare* (*Epist.* 38. 6). For numerous other examples, see A. Otto, *Die Sprichwörter und sprichwörtlichen Redensarten der Römer* (Leipzig 1890) 173 f.

[39] Cf. Matt. 6. 25-32.

[40] Rigault prefers *Gallicos multos* and supports his reading with a reference to Clement of Alexandria, *Paed.* 3. 4. 27. 2, where it is stated that lovers of luxury, besides other superfluous servants, often keep 'many Celts who bear on their shoulders the litters of women.' In *Ad ux.* 2. 8 Tertullian speaks contemptuously of women who marry rich husbands in order to be able to maintain mules and other unbecoming luxuries.

[41] See above, n. 13.

[42] Cf. 1 Cor. 58; Phil. 1. 23.

[43] The harsh, unchristian thoughts of this chapter are repeated in *De exhort. cast.* 12 and *De monog.* 16. On the regard for children among the early Christians, see H. Leclercq's article, *Bonté chrétienne*, DACL 2. 1 (1925) 1008-1054. Further references may be found in E. Plumptre, 'Children,' DCA 1. 351 f.

[44] See above, n. 2. In *De exhort. cast.* 12 Tertullian speaks of

'importunitas liberorum, ad quos suscipiendos *legibus compelluntur homines.*' On the very severe legislation of Augustus in regard to the unmarried and the childless married, and favoring parents with three or more children (*ius trium liberorum*), see also G. Grupp, *Kulturgeschichte der römischen Zeit*, I. Teil: *Die untergehende heidnische Kultur* (2nd ed. Regensburg 1921) 124-32; H. Last, 'The Social Policy of Augustus,' *Cambridge Ancient History* 10 (1934) 441-56; A. Steinwenter, 'Ius liberorum,' RE 10. 2 (1919) 1281-84.

⁴⁵ *Parricidium* is any 'unnatural' murder, especially the murder of a near relative. Tertullian is the first writer to use the words *infanticidium* (*Ad nat.* 1. 15) and *infanticida* (*Apol.* 2, 4). The prevalence of the crime of child murder is often mentioned by the Fathers of the Church, particularly the Apologists. Tertullian writes of it repeatedly. In *De virg. vel.* 14 he speaks of *infantes debellatos a matribus* and in *De an.* 25 describes in detail the instruments used in what he calls the *caecum latrocinium* of infanticide. In our present passage the expression is *parricidiis expugnantur.* For *expugnantur*, Kellner suggests *expunguntur*, a word which graphically pictures an abortion procured by means of the *aeneum spiculum*, a popular method. Cf. the extensive literature listed by Waszink, *De anima* 326 ff. On this whole subject, see I. Giordani, *The Social Message of the Early Church Fathers* (tr. from the Italian by A. Zizzamia, Paterson 1944) 243 ff. and, especially, F. J. Dölger's series of articles under the title 'Das Lebensrecht des ungeborenen Kindes und die Fruchtabtreibung in der Bewertung der heidnischen und christlichen Antike,' AC 4 (1934) 1-61.

⁴⁶ The punctuation adopted here is that of Oehler and Kroymann . . . *expugnantur, nobis demum . . . .* PL 1. 1394 has . . . *parricidiis expugnantur. Nobis quidem . . . .*

⁴⁷ Matt. 24. 19.

⁴⁸ Cf. Luke 21. 23, 25. Both Tertullian and the Vulgate have *pressura.*

⁴⁹ Cf. Luke 17. 27 ff.

⁵⁰ Various interpretations of the text are possible. In the present translation *ab iis* is taken as referring to the *disciplinae divinae* mentioned above. We should then read . . . *Penes Deum, ab iis nos nunc arceant?* There is no manuscript evidence nor editorial authority for *arceant* but it seems as reasonable a conjecture as any. Thelwall and Dodgson both understand *iis* as the antecedent of *quae olim detestabilia.* Kellner feels that *non* may have dropped out before *nos.*

[51] 1 Cor. 7. 29. Tertullian has *Tempus in collecto est* (cf. also *De cultu fem.* 2. 9); the Vulgate, *Tempus breve est.* For this meaning of *collectus*, see Waszink, *De anima* 432.

[52] *Carnem suam obsignant*, lit., 'set a seal upon their flesh.' In *De cultu fem.* 2. 9 Tertullian speaks of 'many who seal themselves to eunuchhood' — *se spadonatui obsignant.*

[53] Lit., 'bath,' 'laver' — *lavacrum*, the normal word among Latin Christians for the sacrament. Regarding the interesting terminology that developed around the word — e. g. *lavacrum novi natalis, mysticum lavacrum, sacrum veniae lavacrum, secundum lavacrum* ('martyrdom,' the 'baptism of blood') etc. — see especially Teeuwen, *op. cit.* 47 f.

[54] Cf. Matt. 19. 12; Tertullian, *De pat.* 13.

[55] *Censeri* in Tertullian is often used for *vocari* or *dici.* See Oehler's note on this passage and on *De cor.* 13.

[56] Cf. Matt. 3. 12. In the temple of Vesta at Rome the goddess was venerated under the symbol of an eternal fire. It is well known that one of the principal duties of the Vestal Virgins was to guard and maintain this flame. Cf. G. Wissowa, *Religion und Kultus der Römer* (2nd ed. Munich 1912) 156-61.

[57] Cf. Apoc. 12. 9 and 20. 2. The phrase *cum ipso dracone* may also be construed with *curantes.* Tertullian speaks similarly of the *auspicia poenarum* when he writes in *De cultu fem.* 2. 6 that those women augur ill for themselves who dye their hair the color of flame; and St. Jerome, in his letter to Laeta on the care of her daughter Paula (*Epist.* 107. 5; cf. Wright, *op. cit.* 351) warns: 'Do not dye her hair red and thereby presage for her the fires of hell.'

[58] Aegium was one of the twelve Achaean cities. It was situated across the gulf of Corinth from Delphi. Pausanias (7. 23 f.) describes this town and its shrines, stating that the temple sacred to Hera (Juno) contained a statue which only women were permitted to look upon.

[59] Cf. Tertullian, *De monog.* 17; *De exhort. cast.* 13.

[60] That is, the pagan priests who serve in the temples of the gods.

[61] Cf. 1 Cor. 15. 53.

[62] If we understand *sustinere* in the sense of 'keep' or 'preserve,' the words *Nobis continentia . . . demonstrata est . . . ad sustinendam novissime voluntatem dei* seem to mean that, according to the teaching of Christ, to practice chastity is to fulfill the will of God. However, the expression *ad sustinendam voluntatem dei* is ambiguous. *Sustinere* in Tertullian frequently has the force of

expectare (cf. *Apol.* 35. 12; *De paen.* 6; *De fuga* 11). In this sense the thought would be that our Lord teaches us continence so that we may more securely wait for the fulfillment of His will at the end of the world (*novissime*). The whole sentence is typical of Tertullian's terse and cryptic style.

⁶³ 1 Cor. 7. 27.

⁶⁴ *Ibid.* 7. 28. There is no explicit reference to widows in this text. St. Paul has been speaking of unmarried men and virgins. He says that all such who marry will have *tribulatio* (*pressura*, Tertullian writes) *carnis* (θλίψιν δὲ τῇ σαρκί). There is no question here of the pain of childbirth, as is clear from the Greek τοιοῦτοι. On the meaning of σάρξ, 'flesh,' in St. Paul, see F. Prat, *The Theology of St. Paul* (tr. by J. L. Stoddard, London 1939) 2. 402.

⁶⁵ St. Paul's teaching on this subject may be found in 1 Tim. 3. 2 and Titus 1. 6. When he writes that the bishop must be a man 'of one wife,' his words are to be taken in a restrictive and not an injunctive sense. Obviously he does not mean that the bishop must be a married man, since he could hardly object if a bishop followed the counsel and example of celibacy which he himself had given. Nor can the old view be taken seriously that St. Paul merely wished to exclude from the episcopacy Greeks who indulged in concubinage and Jews who practiced polygamy. For an attempted defense of this interpretation see H. C. Lea, *A History of Sacerdotal Celibacy* (Philadelphia 1867) 36 f. Tertullian is speaking of successive, not simultaneous, polygamy, and he understands St. Paul to be speaking in the same sense.

Ancient ecclesiastical discipline excluded from the clergy men who were digamists themselves as well as men who were married to digamous women. The latter prescription recalls the legislation of Lev. 21. 7, 14, which forbade a priest to marry a divorced woman or a widow. The history of church law on the subject of digamists and Holy Orders is well summarized by E. Valton, 'Bigamie, irrégularité,' *DTC* 2 (1905) 883-88. — The present Code of Canon Law (c. 984. 4°) states that those who have successively contracted two or more valid marriages are *irregulares ex defectu*. The canon is based on the passages in St. Paul, the constant tradition of the Church, and the feeling that, since marriage represents the union of Christ and the Church, there is something unbecoming in having contracted it more than once.

⁶⁶ Cf. 1 Tim. 5. 9. Widows performed ministerial duties in the Church from apostolic times, as is clear from Acts 6. 1. For an

account of their ministry, see J. Viteau, 'L'institution des diacres et des veuves,' *Rev. d'hist. eccl.* 22 (1926) 513-37; A. Rosambert, *La veuve en droit canonique jusqu'au XIVe siècle* (Paris 1923) 1-113. The patristic texts on widows and widowhood have been collected by J. Mayer, *Monumenta de viduis, diaconissis virginibusque tractantia* (Florilegium patristicum 42, Bonn 1938).

Tertullian appears to speak of the 'ordination' of widows (*adlegi in ordinem*), but their selection was never by the rite of ordination properly so called. This is carefully explained by St. Hippolytus in the *Apostolic Tradition* 11. 1-5: 'When a widow is appointed she is not ordained (χειροτονεῖν) but she shall be chosen by name. . . . Let the widow be instituted by word only. . . . But she shall not be ordained, because she does not offer the oblation nor has she a liturgical ministry (λειτουργία). But ordination is for the clergy on account of their liturgical ministry. But the widow is appointed for prayer, and this is a function of all Christians.' Cf. G. Dix, *The Treatise on the Apostolic Tradition of St. Hippolytus of Rome* (London 1937) 1. 20 f. See also the *Apostolic Constitutions* 8. 25; Rosambert, *op. cit.* 60-62. The word St. Paul uses in 1 Tim. 5. 9 is καταλεγέσθω, i. e. 'let her name be entered on the church roll,' and there is no reason for supposing that Tertullian had anything other than this enrollment in mind.

⁶⁷ Tertullian thinks of the heart of the Christian as an altar from which prayer rises up to God.

⁶⁸ *Tota illa ecclesiae candida de sanctitate conscribitur.* Oehler understands *candida* to mean a 'halo.' On the use of this word as a substantive, see A. d'Alès, 'Candida,' *Rech. de sc. rel.* 3 (1912) 598-600. D'Alès feels that in the present passage *candida* means the saints on earth who will be the future citizens of heaven, thus suggesting the idea of hope and expectation, as it frequently does in Tertullian. Cf. also the excellent observations by Teeuwen, *op. cit.* 97-100.

⁶⁹ The *Pontifex Maximus* held the supreme spiritual authority in the official state religion of Rome. Because of the great importance of the office, the emperors, from the time of Augustus on, reserved it for themselves. This may be why Tertullian speaks of the *Pontifex Maximus* as the *rex saeculi*, though it is more likely that the reference here is merely to the supreme pontiff as the ruler of heathendom. In the early days at Rome the *Pontifex Maximus* was not permitted to leave Italy, was not to look upon a corpse, was obliged to have a wife without reproach and could not marry a second time.

The emperors certainly did not consider themselves bound by such restrictions. Cf. Wissowa, *op. cit.* 508-513.

70 *Affectare* in the sense of 'feign' or 'simulate' is post-Augustan. In *De praesc. haer.* 40, Tertullian gives other examples of pagan practices which he says are diabolical imitations of the Christian mysteries, especially those of baptism and the Eucharist.

71 Isa. 1. 17 f. Commentators are not in complete accord on the interpretation of the first part of verse 18. The difficulty is whether the words which Tertullian gives as *Venite disputemus* are to be connected with the thought of the preceding verses or are to be taken with the thought which follows. The Hebrew expression 'let us reason together,' is a legal one and here refers to the quasi-trial at law between Jahweh and the people which forms the preface of the prophecy. The people have come to present their case to Jahweh, but their sins have made their prayer unacceptable. They must first perform works of justice and charity, then let them bring their case to court. Cf. E. J. Kissane, *The Book of Isaiah* 1 (Dublin 1941) 12. Tertullian's Latin is closer to the original Hebrew and the Greek of the Septuagint than is the Vulgate's *venite arguite me*.

72 Tertullian expresses the same thought in *De virg. vel.* 10; cf. also Cyprian, *De bono pat.* 20 (*patientia . . . tuetur in virginibus beatam integritatem, in viduis laboriosam castitatem*); Jerome, *Ad Geruchiam de monogamia: Epist.* 123. 10.

73 *Quae a Domino indulgentur, sua gratia gubernantur; quae ab homine captantur, studio perpetrantur. Sua* is best taken with its logical subject. *Captare* means more in this context than 'to seek' or 'to strive after,' the more usual sense of the word and the one adopted by Thelwall and Dodgson. To keep the parallelism with the thought of the preceding sentence and with the word *indulgentur* in this sentence, we must understand that the objects of one's efforts are actually attained. Kellner appreciates this when he translates, '. . . was aber vom Menschen ergriffen wird. . . .'

The apparent implication that the chastity of widows is not due to the grace of God but is exclusively the result of their own efforts might be taken to be an adumbration of Pelagianism. However, the expressions '. . . we have of our own efforts (*sunt . . . nostrae operationis*)' and '. . . won at the cost of personal endeavor (*studio perpetrantur*)' may be understood in an affirmative sense and are not necessarily to be taken in an exclusive one. In such texts, *libertatis nostrae admonemur*, says the Council of Trent (cf. ES 797). We must not interpret Tertullian's words in too technical a sense. There is no detailed study of the nature of grace, the mystery of its distribution and its relation to man's free will until St. Augustine. For Tertullian's teaching on the subject, see d'Alès, *op. cit.* 268 ff.

[74] Tertullian here quotes one of the several passages in which St. Paul borrows from, or alludes to, classical authors: 1 Cor. 15. 33, which is indebted to the comic poet Menander. Tertullian's indifference to verbal accuracy or verbal consistency in citing Scripture is illustrated by his translation of ὁμιλίαι κακαί as *congressus mali* in the present passage and as *confabulationes malae* a few chapters later; cf. below, 2. 3.

[75] Phil. 3. 19 and compare 1 Tim. 5. 13. St. Jerome, in his celebrated letter to Eustochium (*Epist.* 22. 29), has a somewhat similar passage. He writes: 'Cast from you like the plague those idle and inquisitive virgins and widows who go about to married women's houses and surpass the very parasites in a play by their unblushing effrontery. "Evil communications corrupt good manners," and these women care for nothing but their belly and its adjacent members.' Cf. F. A. Wright, *op. cit.* 123.

[76] Tertullian seems to consider remarriage after divorce as no more reprehensible than remarriage after the death of a spouse. This need not mean, however, that he allows the dissolution of a *matrimonium ratum et consummatum*. Le Prieur's note on this passage, ML 1. 1402, is misleading. It is quite possible that there is question here of Christian women who were baptized *after* their marriage, and subsequently divorced by their pagan husbands. If so, they might be allowed to marry again, by an application of what we now call the Pauline privilege. This would explain Tertullian's insistence that the second marriage must be, as the Apostle says, *only in the Lord*, i. e. contracted with another Christian. In other passages his position on divorce and remarriage is stated with greater precision. For example, in *De monog.* 11 he declares that the permission to remarry granted by St. Paul in 1 Cor. 7. 39 is restricted to those who are free *per mortem utique, non per repudium . . . quia repudiatis non permitteret nubere adversus pristinum praeceptum*. Tertullian constantly insists on the unity and indissolubility of the marriage bond and, as a Montanist, his error *per excessum* lay in contending that it was not broken even by death. It is safe to conclude with d'Alès, *op. cit.* 465, that '. . . il garde intact le mérite d'avoir constamment affirmé l'indissolubilité du lien conjugal.' Cf. also J. Delazer, 'De insolubilitate matrimonii juxta Tertullianum,' *Antonianum* 7 (1932) 441-64.

[77] 1 Cor. 7. 39. In the following chapter he explains the phrase *in Domino* as meaning *in nomine Domini, quod indubitate est Christiano.*

[78] This, possibly, is the circumstance related at the beginning of the following chapter.

[79] Cf. 1 Cor. 7. 8.

[80] Here Tertullian writes *tantum in Domino*, a correct translation of the Greek. In his earlier quotation of the text he has *potissimum in Domino.*

[81] The expression, *nuptias suas de Ecclesia tolleret*, probably has reference to a marriage contracted by a Christian woman with a pagan without the sanction or blessing of the Church. The ancient Church did not outlaw such clandestine marriages, although in as early a writer as Ignatius of Antioch we read: 'For those of both sexes who contemplate marriage, it is proper to enter the union with the sanction of the bishop': *Epist. ad Polycarpum* 5 (tr. by J. A. Kleist, ACW 1. 98). Tertullian seems to have felt strongly on the subject. In *De pud.* 4 he asserts that *occultae conjugationes, id est non prius apud Ecclesiam professae, iuxta moechiam et fornicationem periclitantur.* Cf. below, n. 143 and n. 146 to *De monog.* For the history of ecclesiastical intervention in Christian marriage, see G. H. Joyce, *Christian Marriage* (2nd ed. London 1948) 37 ff., and T. A. Lacey, *Marriage in Church and State* (New York 1912) 108 ff.

[82] 1 Cor. 7. 12-14.

[83] It was the constant teaching of the Fathers and early Church councils that Christians should avoid mixed marriages. St. Ambrose says very simply (*De Abr.* 1. 9): 'There can be no unity of love where there is no unity of faith.' The prescription was, no doubt, often violated, though St. Jerome is probably exaggerating when he writes (*Adv. Iov.* 1. 10) that the greater number (*pleraeque*) of Christian women in his day despise the Apostle's command and marry heathens. On the entire problem of mixed marriages in the early Church, see J. Köhne, *Die Ehen zwischen Christen und Heiden in den ersten christlichen Jahrhunderten* (Paderborn 1931), esp. 27-66. For Ambrose, see W. J. Dooley, *Marriage according to St. Ambrose* (SCA 11, Washington 1948) 82 89.

[84] 1 Cor. 7. 15.

[85] *Ibid.* 7. 17.

[86] The point of this final argument may appear from the following paraphrase. Those who are called to the faith are those who were pagans. They are called in peace. They would not be so called if

they were obliged to break up their marriage after their conversion. Hence, Christians who were married before they embraced the faith may continue to live with their pagan consorts. Therefore, St. Paul in this passage is thinking exclusively of persons who are already married. Consequently, his words may not be understood as extending a general permission to all Christians to marry pagans. Tertullian's delight in dialectic is illustrated by his use of so elaborate an argument to dispose of so empty an exegetical error.

[87] 1 Cor. 7. 39.

[88] *Retractare* not infrequently in Tertullian means 'to doubt,' 'to find a difficulty,' 'to have misgivings'; cf. H. Hoppe, *Syntax und Stil des Tertullian* (Leipzig 1903) 138.

[89] Kroymann believes that this sentence is a gloss representing an indignant question: 'What could there be any doubt about? The Holy Spirit has spoken!' Other editors, in place of *spiritus*, have *Christus* or *apostolus*.

[90] Tertullian implies that St. Paul and the Holy Spirit are joined as one cause in the composition of this epistle. The close identification leads to a confusion of subject in the clause *qui nos ad exemplum suum hortatur* (1 Cor. 7. 7). For Tertullian's teaching on the inspiration of Scripture, see d'Alès, *op. cit.* 221 ff.

[91] *Inter eum qui.* . . . The prescription against mixed marriages binds both men and women. The variant reading, *inter eam qui*, can hardly be admitted.

[92] Here the role of the Holy Spirit is merely one of assistance; it is not that of a principal cause.

[93] Kroymann has reordered the wording of this sentence. If *omnino* is taken with *disiungi* rather than with *non contrahi* (*Agobardinus*, Oehler, etc.), we might possibly see a reference to perfect divorce as distinct from a divorce *a mensa et toro*.

[94] *Nisi stupri causa* instead of the Vulgate's *nisi fornicationis causa*, Matt. 5. 32, 19. 9. For a synopsis of the various interpretations of this difficult clause and the meaning of the word πορνεία, cf. J. P. Haran, 'The Indissolubility of Christian Marriage,' *Theol. Stud.* 2 (1941) 198-220, and U. Holzmeister, 'Die Streitfrage über die Ehescheidungstexte bei Matthaeus,' *Biblica* 26 (1945) 133-46. J. Bonsirven, in a valuable chapter of his work, *Le divorce dans le Nouveau Testament* (Paris 1948), has compiled and analyzed the patristic passages which bear on the exegesis of the two texts. He concludes (p. 68) that Tertullian 'pense que l'incise ne permet qu' une separation provisoire; il faut attendre la conversion, toujours

possible, du conjoint coupable, dont on a dû se séparer pour ne pas participer à son péché.'

⁹⁵ Tertullian's first answer to the objection is a denial of parity. Our Lord's rejection of divorce is so absolute that not even the danger of defilement is a sufficient reason for breaking off the marriage. Thus it is possible for one man to be at fault for marrying and another to be at fault for divorcing a pagan woman. It must be admitted that the viewpoint expressed here is not sympathetic to the Pauline privilege. Tertullian has chosen to ignore the important words: *Quod si infidelis discedit, discedat* (1 Cor. 7. 15).

⁹⁶ The text is corrupt. The argument, however, appears to be this: the grace of God, given the Christian at the moment of conversion, sanctifies the unconverted pagan spouse by a kind of concomitance. If the pagan is not actually joined in marriage to the Christian at the time of the latter's conversion, this concomitant grace cannot be received. Grace effects sanctification only when it finds the conditions present which are necessary for its reception. The fallacy in the argument is the assumption that because St. Paul affirms the fact of sanctification in the one case (that is, the case in which conversion takes place after marriage; and this is the interpretation which Tertullian puts on 1 Cor. 7. 12-14), he denies its possibility in all others.

⁹⁷ 1 Cor. 5. 11.

⁹⁸ *Die illo* (Matt. 24. 36, Mark 13. 32, etc.) for *dillo* of the *Agobardinus*. Oehler, following Rhenan and all other early editors, reads *de illo*. Cf. G. Thörnell, *Studia Tertullianea* 3 (Uppsala 1922) 38 f.

⁹⁹ Cf. 1 Cor. 3. 16.

¹⁰⁰ Cf. *ibid*. 6. 15. The Vulgate has *meretricis*, Tertullian *adulterae*. Oehler understands these sentences not as rhetorical questions (Kroymann) but as an imaginary defense offered by the guilty before the tribunal of God.

¹⁰¹ Cf. *ibid*. 6. 19 f.

¹⁰² A possible reference to one of the spiritual directors mentioned at the beginning of the preceding chapter.

¹⁰³ On the distinction between mortal and venial sin according to the mind of Tertullian, see H. L. Motry, *The Concept of Mortal Sin in Early Christian Literature* (Washington 1920) 41-124.

¹⁰⁴ In ch. 2.

¹⁰⁵ Cf. Matt. 6. 24.

[106] The word used is *exstructionem*. Compare Juvenal, *Sat.* 6. 502, *altum aedificat caput*.

[107] In the ancient Church a 'station day' was a day of special religious observance, specifically a day of prayer and fasting. For a brief explanation of the etymology of the word *statio* and its transference to 'station churches' see H. Leclercq's article 'Station Days,' CE 14. 268 f.; Teeuwen, *op. cit.* 101-120; and the literature listed by Waszink, *op. cit.* 513 f.

[108] On the moral problems which arose for Christians from the practice of public bathing, see H. Dumaine, 'Bains,' DACL 2. 1 (1925) 72-117; also J. Zellinger, *Bad und Bäder in der altchristlichen Kirche* (Munich 1928) 34 ff.

[109] Tertullian often uses *denique* in this sense; cf. TLL 5. 533. For a detailed description of the ceremonies on Easter Eve, see L. Duchesne, *Origines du culte chrétien* (5th ed. Paris 1925) 252-71.

[110] The Apologists frequently refer to these calumnies: cf., e. g., Tertullian, *Apol.* 7 f. and *Ad nat.* 1. 15 f.; Minucius Felix, *Oct.* 9. The principal accusations were that on these occasions the Christians celebrated Thyestean banquets and indulged in orgies of incest. — For the use of *dominicus* ('consecrated to the Lord' or 'Sunday') see F. J. Dölger, 'Zu *dominica sollemnia* bei Tertullianus,' AC 6 (1940) 108-115; also the literature cited by Waszink, *op. cit.* 167.

[111] The kiss of peace, as a natural sign of love and harmony, was widely used in the ancient Church, both in ordinary salutations and as a part of liturgical worship. Abuses which sometimes attended the practice are mentioned by Athenagoras, *Suppl.* 32, and Clement of Alexandria, *Paed.* 3. 11. 81.

[112] Cf. 1 Tim. 5. 10. On the ceremony of washing the feet of the newly baptized, see especially St. Ambrose, *De myst.* 6. 31-33, *De sacr.* 3. 1. 4-7, and the literature quoted by J. Quasten in the edition of these texts, *Monumenta eucharistica et liturgica vetustissima* (Bonn 1936) 128 f., 152. For the origin of this liturgical rite, see E. J. Duncan, *Baptism in the Demonstrations of Aphraates the Persian Sage* (SCA 8, Washington 1945) 70-74.

[113] There is some dispute over Tertullian's position on the *disciplina arcani*. See the extensive literature in P. Batiffol, *Etudes d'histoire et de théologie positive* 1 (7th ed. Paris 1926) 1-41. In spite of passages like the present, Batiffol believes that Tertullian was not too insistent on the strict observance of such a law.

[114] Cf. Matt. 1. 1-6, 25-34.

[115] Matt. 7. 6.

[116] *Corpusculum*, as a term of endearment. T. R. Glover, *The Conflict of Religions in the Early Roman Empire* (London 1927) 314, suggests that expressions such as these reveal a tenderness and humanity in Tertullian's character which have not been fully appreciated. — The Sign of the Cross is a Christian usage of great antiquity. It was made originally with the thumb of the right hand, usually on the forehead, although the practice of tracing the sign on the lips and over the heart is not infrequently mentioned. Sometimes the thumb was laid crosswise over the index finger and kissed; again, the sign was traced in the air with a finger or with the whole hand. The custom also existed of signing with a cross such objects as altars, chalices, food, drink, and, as Tertullian mentions here, the bed, probably immediately before retiring (compare Prudentius, *Cath.* 6. 129). By the ninth century the primitive use of signing the forehead with a single cross was supplanted, rather generally among the people, by a form which approximates that which we know in the West today, although it was not until the thirteenth century that the Latin church adopted the Sign of the Cross in which the left shoulder is touched before the right.

In Christian antiquity the Sign of the Cross was used on various occasions and for various purposes (cf. Tertullian, *De cor. mil.* 3 and *De res. car.* 8): as a blessing, to denote membership in the church, as an exorcism, as a reminder and encouragement in time of trials and afflictions, as a safeguard against disease or accident, as a remedy against temptation, in the administration of the sacraments, and in other sacred ceremonies. For further details, see J. Sauer's article, 'Kreuzzeichen,' LTK 6. 265-67, and H. Leclercq, 'Signe de la Croix,' DACL 3. 3139-44; on the present passage, cf. Köhne, *op. cit.* 52 f.

[117] This was a popular exorcism in the early Church; see F. J. Dölger, AC 3 (1932) 192-203; also ACW 10. 116 n. 146. Tertullian says that evil spirits depart *afflatu nostro* (*Apol.* 23), and in the *De idololatria* (11) he speaks with approval of the practice of spitting and hissing at pagan altars. Liturgical insufflation found use especially in baptism and it remains part of the rite today.

[118] This charge was frequently made against the Christians. Suetonius (*Nero* 16) described them as a *gens hominum superstitionis maleficae*, and St. Ambrose (*Epist.* 1) relates that when St. Agnes stood before her judge, the crowd cried out against her, *Tolle magam! Tolle maleficam!* The ritual of the Christians, known and rumored, their secretiveness ('silent in public, garrulous in corners,' Minucius

Felix, *Oct.* 8), the miracles they spoke about or performed, their courage under torture, practices such as those Tertullian mentions in this context, all contributed to the spread of this belief.

[119] There are numerous references in early Christian writers to the practice of reserving the Eucharist privately after the public celebration of the mysteries in the church. Thus Tertullian (*De orat.* 19) uses the words *accepto corpore Domini et reservato.* In the present passage his words imply a frequent reception of Holy Communion at home. They also give valuable testimony to the ancient practice of receiving the Eucharist while fasting. For Tertullian's teaching on the real presence, cf. G. Rauschen, *Eucharist and Penance in the First Six Centuries of the Church* (tr. from the 2nd ed., St. Louis 1913) 11 ff., and the literature there listed.

[120] Bread dipped in the blood of a murdered baby. Cf. the references in n. 110, especially *Apol.* 8: . . . *excipe rudem sanguinem, eo panem tuum satia . . .* ; and . . . *panis quo sanguinis iurulentiam colligas. . . .* See F. J. Dölger, '*Sacramentum infanticidii,*' AC 4 (1934) 226.

[121] It is not clear just how such husbands . . . *dotes . . . mercedem silentii faciant.* The whole passage is very difficult and has been variously interpreted.

[122] Reading *laboribus* (for *laribus*) *alienis*, with the *Agobardinus.*

[123] For a brief account of the Roman religious calendar, see Seyffert-Nettleship-Sandys, *A Dictionary of Classical Antiquities* (London 1894) under the words *fasti* and *feriae.*

[124] The pagan custom of adorning private homes with laurel and lamps on festal days seems to have been particularly odious to Tertullian. He speaks of it at length in the *De idololatria* (15), and in the *Apologeticum* (35) he condemns those who on public occasions think it the proper thing . . . *induere domui . . . habitum alicuius novi lupanaris* (cf. also Juvenal 6. 79, 227 and 12. 91). See especially K. Baus, *Der Kranz in Antike und Christentum* (Theophaneia 2, Bonn 1940) 66-69.

[125] 1 Cor. 6. 2.

[126] Cf. Tertullian, *Apol.* 39. 2.

[127] On this whole passage see Köhne, *op. cit.* 58. f.

[128] That is, the hope of winning over their husbands to the faith; cf. 1 Cor. 7. 16 f. and 1 Peter 3. 1.

[129] Theologians regularly cite this passage in developing the patristic proof for the sacramental nature of marriage, and the words, *habens iam ex parte divinae gratiae patrocinium,* do seem to imply

that there is some sort of title to grace conferred in marriage. A difficulty, however, is caused by the consideration that in the present instance this grace is apparently thought of as being due to conversion and baptism rather than to the exchange of matrimonial consent. Moreover, the argument proves too much, since it is the more common opinion today that in a marriage of the kind described here the convert to Christianity does not receive the sacrament of matrimony. Cf. C. Boyer, *op. cit.* 41.

    [130] For the word *magnalia* (μεγαλεῖα), 'miracles,' later replaced by *virtutes* (δυνάμεις), cf. ACW 3. 139 n. 304.

    [131] The expression is *dei candidatus.* Compare *diaboli candidatus* (*De cor. mil.* 7) and *angelorum candidati* (*De orat.* 3).

    [132] Reading *petitoribus*, with Kroymann and the majority of manuscripts.

    [133] *Dispector*: cf. Tertullian, *De an.* 15. 4, and Waszink *ad loc.*

    [134] For the interpretation of this clause, see H. Hoppe, *Beiträge zur Sprache und Kritik Tertullians* (Lund 1932) 26.

    [135] The phrasing of this decree (*Senatusconsultum Claudianum*) is given in Tacitus, *Ann.* 12. 53. It had reference to freeborn women who cohabited with slaves. If the slave's master refused consent to the union, the woman became his slave; if he consented, she was to be considered in the position of a freedwoman. Tertullian has the masculine *servituti vindicandos*, but he is often careless of, or indifferent to, gender. In the next sentence he writes . . . *extraneis iunctae libertatem suam amittant.* The attitude of the Church to such unions is revealed by the well-known passage in Hippolytus, *Philosoph.* 9. 7, where one of the major counts in the indictment against Callistus is the charge that he permitted the marriage of free women and slaves. In the eyes of the state such unions were mere *contubernia*; in the eyes of the Church they were valid marriages. Thus the text is particularly important as illustrating the early ecclesiastical claim to jurisdiction over Christian marriage, at least in the matter of determining impediments.

    [136] Cf. 1 Cor. 7. 39. In this sentence *a Domino . . . denuntiatum* is suggested by *dominorum denuntiationem* two or three sentences above, although the parallelism is not exact.

    [137] *Matrona.*

    [138] Compare Matt. 19. 23 f.; Mark 10. 23 f.; Luke 18. 24 f.

    [139] The word used here is *cinerarii.* Hairdressers were so called because they heated their curling irons in ashes or glowing coals. Cf. above, n. 40.

[140] Rigault notes that in such unions *maior licentia datur feminis, cum abortivo non est opus*, and he quotes St. Jerome's remark (*Adv. Iovin.* 1. 47) that in affairs of this kind *habetur secura libido*. Cf. also Juvenal 6. 366 ff., and Martial 6. 67. Kroymann considers this interpretation ingenious but improbable. He conjectures *se⟨le⟩ctis* for *sectis ad licentiam*.

[141] Cf. Matt. 5. 3 or, better, Luke 6. 20, since St. Matthew has 'Blessed are the poor *in spirit*' while St. Luke and Tertullian omit this important qualification.

[142] Tertullian points out that Christian and pagan marriage, although superficially similar, are actually profoundly different. In five specific details, using technical legal expressions proper to the Roman religious-civil ceremony, he shows how, in the Christian celebration of marriage, the supernatural replaces the natural in each instance. The passage is one of the most valuable in early Christian literature on the sacred nature of marriage and the Church's role in its celebration. Moreover, it is not until the well-known *Responsa ad Bulgaros* of Nicholas I in the ninth century (cf. Mansi 15. 402) that we have a more detailed description of the marriage rite in the Latin Church. For a further discussion of this subject, see L. Duchesne, *op. cit.* 428 ff. He shows that the ancient Roman marriage ritual was preserved in almost all of its details in the Christian ceremony.

[143] *Quam Ecclesia conciliat*: among the Romans one who brought about or arranged a marriage was called a *conciliator* (cf. Nepos, *Atticus* 12. 2). In a Christian marriage the place of the *conciliator* is taken by the officers of the Church, bishops, priests, deacons, etc. The precise nature of their intervention is not clear in all its details, but see above, n. 81, and *De monog.* 11.

[144] The words are *et confirmat oblatio*. In a Roman wedding, on the morning of their marriage, the bride and groom, at one point in the ritual, addressed a prayer to the gods of marriage and offered a sacrifice, usually at one of the public altars. In a marriage by *confarreatio* the offering was one of fruits and a wheaten loaf. At a later period is was more usual to offer a bloody sacrifice. For Christians this ceremony was replaced by the offering of the Eucharistic sacrifice. Some authorities have denied that *oblatio* has reference to the Mass, but in the present context it is difficult to see what other natural meaning the word can have. Cf. d'Alès, *op. cit.* 308, 376; Köhne, *op. cit.* 69 f.

[145] The blessing of the bishop or priest does not constitute the

essence of Christian marriage but is an official seal placed upon it after the contract is completed (*obsignat benedictio*). This corresponds to the seal placed upon the written marriage settlements in the Roman ceremonial. The identification of the sacrament of marriage with the nuptial blessing was a theological error attended with the most serious consequences at a later period in the Church's history.

[146] Cf. Gen. 2. 24; Matt. 19. 6; 1 Cor. 6. 16.

[147] Literally, 'they prostrate themselves together' (*volutantur*). Compare *Adv. Marc.* 3. 18, '. . . *genibus depositis et manibus caedentibus pectus et facie humi volutante orationem commendare* . . . ,' and *Apol.* 40. 15, '. . . *in sacco et cinere volutantes . . . Deum tangimus.*' On the various positions assumed by the early Christians in public and private prayer, and on the identification of prostration and genuflection, see H. Leclercq, 'Genuflexion,' DACL 6. 1. 1017-21.

[148] The expression is *sacrificia sine scrupulo*. The freedom enjoyed in a marriage between two Christians is contrasted point by point with the difficulties of a mixed marriage as these difficulties were described in earlier chapters.

[149] The word *gratulatio* may mean 'thanksgiving' as well as 'greeting.' In *De an.* 1. 3 Tertullian uses it as the equivalent of *gaudium*, 'joy,' and this is a possible meaning in the present passage also.

[150] Cf. Eph. 5. 19 and Col. 3. 16.

[151] Cf. Matt. 18. 20.

[152] 'Only in the Lord'; cf. above, ch. 2.

AN EXHORTATION TO CHASTITY

INTRODUCTION

[1] References to earlier literature on the subject may be found in O. Bardenhewer, *op. cit.*, 2. 395. For a study of the date of the *De exhortatione castitatis* in its relationship to the *Ad uxorem* and the *De monogamia*, see G. N. Bonwetsch, *Die Schriften Tertullians nach der Zeit ihrer Abfassung untersucht* (Bonn 1878) 57-61. The dates given here, 204 and 212 A. D., represent *termini ante* and *post quem non*, according to a consensus of estimates given by various modern patrologists.

[2] The word *castitas* may be taken as synonymous with *continentia*, here in the title and throughout the treatise. See TLL 3. 542.

³ St. Jerome (*Adv. Iov.* 1.13) refers to a work *De molestiis nuptiarum*, now lost, written when Tertullian was still a young man. For some interesting comments on Tertullian's attitude to women, marriage and the family, cf. Monceaux, *op. cit.* 1.387. He writes: ' Ce grand ennemi du mariage était marié, naturellement.'

⁴ *Ad ux.* 1.2 f.; 2.8.

⁵ Cf. *Adv. Marc.* 1.29; 5.7, 15; also Preisker, *op. cit.* 197. Compare, too, *De res. carn.* 5, and *De carne Chr.* 4. On the difference between the basic principles of Montanist and Marcionite asceticism, see P. de Labriolle, *La crise Montaniste* 396. It may be said, in general, that the Montanists warned against marriage because of their belief in the proximity of the parousia; the Marcionites rejected it absolutely because of their belief that it was established by the creator-god of the Old Testament and, accordingly, must be considered as something evil in itself.

⁶ *De an.* 27.4. In 11.4 of the same treatise Tertullian speaks of the 'ecstatic vision' of Adam, 'wherein he prophesied that great sacrament in Christ and in the Church.'

⁷ d'Alès, *op. cit.* 370.

TEXT

¹ It is impossible to discover the identity of the person to whom this exhortation is addressed. Possibly Tertullian is merely using a literary device and has no definite individual in mind. It is worth noting, however, that his ascetical ideals are not proposed to women only.

² The Latin is *de exitu singularitatis cogitare*. The translation takes *exitus* as the equivalent of *sors* or *exitium*, and *singularitatis* as an appositional genitive. The expression might also mean ' you are thinking about putting an end to your loneliness by remarriage.' In this case, *exitus* would be synonymous with *finis*, and *singularitatis* would be taken as an objective genitive.

³ 1 Thess. 4.3.

⁴ Cf. Gen. 1.26: *Faciamus hominem ad imaginem et similitudinem nostram.* Tertullian seems to think of *imago* as suggesting a resemblance in the order of nature and *similitudo* a resemblance in the order of grace. Compare *De bap.* 5, and Irenaeus, *Adv. haer.* 5.6.1 (Harvey). There is no basis for this distinction in the Hebrew text and the reduplication there is used merely for the sake of emphasis. Cf. P. Heinisch, *Das Buch Genesis* (Bonn 1930) 101,

and I. Hübscher, *De imagine Dei in homine viatore* (Louvain 1932) 5.

⁵ Cf. Lev. 11. 44; 19. 2; 1 Peter 1. 16.

⁶ The second and third degrees of chastity or continence as described here are not distinguished so carefully as we might wish. It may seem that a widow or widower who continues to live a single life would also be practicing the chastity of monogamy as Tertullian defines it. However, he is interested particularly in giving the *terminus a quo* of the three degrees and, from this viewpoint, his distinction is clear enough: some persons practice continence from birth, some from the time of their baptism and some, though they continue to use marriage after baptism, do not remarry if they lose their consorts by death.

⁷ Cf. Matt. 10. 29.

⁸ Job 1. 21.

⁹ This same argument is used in *Ad ux.* 1. 7 and *De monog.* 9.

¹⁰ The objection, which occasions a lengthy, involved and tendentious digression on the will of God, is that if everything happens *because* God wills it, it follows that even second marriage is according to His will, if and when it is actually contracted. The problem which Tertullian touches in his solution is that of reconciling God's *concursus* and man's freedom, especially with reference to the question of moral evil. The passage is of interest, not because of any unique, intrinsic value in the solution proposed, but because it represents one of the earliest attempts by a Christian writer to come to grips with the problem *de auxiliis*. It may be said, in general, that Tertullian tends to stress man's freedom and responsibility rather than the efficacy of divine grace; but cf. above, n. 73 to *Ad ux.* For a further discussion of this question, particularly in its relationship to dualism, see V. Naumann's careful study, 'Das Problem des Bösen in Tertullians zweitem Buch gegen Marcion,' *Zeitschr. f. kath. Theol.* 58 (1934) 311-63; 533-51.

¹¹ The very existence of such sanctions proves that man is a free and responsible agent in choosing to observe or violate the commandments of God.

¹² Ecclus. 15. 18. In the Vulgate this verse does not include the words *gustasti enim de agnitionis arbore.* It may be that Tertullian intends them as an explanatory note of his own and not as part of the quotation. They are suggested by Gen. 2. 9 and 3. 17.

¹³ The text is corrupt and the translation follows Oehler's version (*Ceterum voluntas Dei in obaudientiam venerat*). The sense appears

to be that if God had no will in the matter there would be no question of obedience or disobedience. Kroymann conjectures *Ceterum voluntas ⟨ei de⟩ dei inobaudientia venerat*, which appears to mean that Adam's bad will was in some way the *result* of his disobedience. Possibly the best interpretation of the words would be, reading *in obaudientiam* rather than *inobaudientia*, that what *God* willed was Adam's obedience, whatever one say about the devil's activity and Adam's own choice. A synopsis of Tertullian's teaching on original sin may be found in d'Alès, *op. cit.* 120-27 and 264-68; see also R. Roberts, *The Theology of Tertullian* (London 1924) 162 f.

[14] Cf. Gen. 2. 17.

[15] Even though God's will is made known to us, we must still investigate whether what He wills is willed positively or merely permissively, absolutely or conditionally.

[16] Reading with Kroymann and earlier editors, against Oehler, . . . *non purae voluntatis*. If the negative is not inserted, we shall find it difficult to say what the *prima species purae voluntatis* would be. The uncertainty might be removed by translating *pura voluntas* as ' manifest will,' although this forces the sense of the adjective and raises new contextual difficulties. The point of the whole passage seems to be this: God has an absolute will and a mixed, or conditional, will. The mixed will is of two kinds: first, it is a permissive will, i. e. a will of toleration; God *tolerates* a course of action which He does not absolutely will. The second kind of mixed will is not one of toleration, but is concerned with things that must be done. Now, even among these there are some actions which He *prefers* to others. Second marriage is according to God's will of toleration; refusal to marry a second time is according to His preferential will. In neither case is there a question of God's absolute will.

[17] *Ex parte delinquis.* For Tertullian's use of *delictum* in the sense of *peccatum*, see TLL 5. 459, *s. v.* St. Augustine, *Quaest, in Hept.* 3. 20, says that *peccatum* may be considered as *perpetratio mali* and *delictum* as *desertio boni*.

[18] Therefore, in neither case can those who marry a second time rightfully claim that they are acting according to the will of God: first, because indulgence is a kind of unwilling volition; second, because when God indicates a preference, He equivalently rescinds a permission.

[19] Cf. 1 Cor. 7. 6. After having labored to show that an indulgence on God's part is an unwilling volition, Tertullian is rather

inconsistent in reminding us that in the matter of second marriage the indulgence is not really God's at all.

20 1 Cor. 7. 9 f.

21 There is no evidence in the text that St. Paul has a restriction such as this in mind.

22 Cf. Ad ux. 1. 3.

23 Cf. n. 20 to Ad ux.

24 Tertullian is unable to see, or unwilling to admit, that a thing can be 'good' and 'less good' at the same time. Whether or not marriage is an absolute good in itself, is a distinct question and one to be decided on its own merits, as it is in other passages of St. Paul, notably Eph. 5. 25-32.

25 1 Cor. 7. 27 f.

26 Ibid. 7. 25.

27 Cf. ibid. 28, 29, 32-34.

28 The amazing sophistry and illogical reasoning of such arguments are difficult to excuse in a writer of Tertullian's ability. As he approached his extreme Montanist position, however, it became increasingly difficult for him to discover valid arguments for the opinions he held. At the same time, his judgment about the worth of an argument became increasingly warped by his fanatical asceticism. He is in the pathetic position of an old crusader fighting for an impossible cause, as well as an unworthy one.

29 1 Cor. 7. 39 f.

30 The verb figulare and the substantive figulatio occur only in Tertullian.

31 Cf. n. 7 to Ad ux.

32 The subject of inquit is not expressed. In Gen. 2. 24 it appears to be Adam who says, 'They will be two in one flesh.' Christ makes the words His own in Matt. 19. 5 and Mark 10. 8. They are also found in 1 Cor. 6. 16 and Eph. 5. 31. Tertullian evidently believes that they were first spoken 'prophetically' by Adam (that is, God spoke through Adam's lips) while in ecstasy. Compare De ieiun. 3 and De an. 11 and 21.

33 For this use of semel in Tertullian, see the references in Hoppe, op. cit. 111.

34 Cf. Eph. 5. 32. Tertullian's use of in with the accusative (. . . apostolus in ecclesiam et Christum interpretatur . . .) is closer to the Greek εἰς Χριστὸν καὶ εἰς τὴν ἐκκλησίαν than is the Vulgate's . . . ego autem dico in Christo et in ecclesia.

35 Sacramentum = μυστήριον. For the meaning of the term in St.

Paul, cf. Prat, *op. cit.*, 272. There is, of course, no argument for
the existence of the sacrament of marriage from the mere use of the
word *sacramentum* in Eph. 5. 32. When Tertullian speaks of marriage as 'Christ's sacrament,' he understands the word in the same
sense it has in this passage of St. Paul: that is, marriage is called
a sacrament because it has a mystical signification in relationship to
(εἰς or *in*; cf. the preceding note) the union of Christ and His
church. See also, in this connection, *De an.* 11 and, especially, *Adv.
Marc.* 5. 18. — There has been considerable discussion about the
meaning of *sacramentum* in Tertullian. Cf. E. de Backer, *Sacramentum. Le mot et l'idée représentée par lui dans les oeuvres de
Tertullien* (Louvain 1911); J. de Ghellinck (with E. de Backer,
J. Poukens, G. Lebacqz), *Pour l'histoire du mot 'Sacramentum'*;
1. *Les anténicéens* (Louvain 1924) 59 — 152; A. Kolping, *Sacramentum Tertullianeum. Erster Teil: Untersuchungen über die Anfänge
des christlichen Gebrauches der Vokabel sacramentum* (Münster
i. W. 1948); H. Bornkamm, ' μυστήριον,' TWNT 4 (1940) 809-834.
D'Alès, *op. cit.* 322 ff., gives numerous examples of the word in its
significance of 'symbol' or 'mystery' and shows how, in this sense,
Tertullian uses it of the sacraments of baptism, confirmation, the
Eucharist and marriage. Regarding μυστήριον- *sacramentum* and the
sacraments, see also O. Casel, *Das christliche Kultmysterium* (3rd ed.
Freiburg i. Br. 1948), and especially numerous articles in the *Jahr-
buch für Liturgiewissenschaft* (1921-1941). Cf. also the useful nota-
tions in A. Souter, *A Glossary of Later Latin to 600 A. D.* (Oxford
1949) 360.

[36] The sentence reads: *In utraque degenerat is, qui de monogamia
exorbitat. Degenerare* means, originally, to depart from one's race or
kind and this meaning is retained here.

[37] Gen. 4. 19. Lamech was descended from Cain and thus, medi-
ately, polygamy is *a maledicto viro.*

[38] In his exegesis Tertullian favors a literal, realistic interpretation
of Scripture. Cf. *Ad ux.* n. 9. Occasionally, as in the present
instance, he appeals to a typical sense, but not always too success-
fully. Thus, he tells us here that the multiple marriages of the
Patriarchs are types and symbols, but fails to say what it is that they
prefigure. In *Ad ux.* 1. 2 and *De monog.* 4, 6 he gives different
solutions to the problem of polygamy in the Old Law.

[39] Gen. 1. 28.

[40] 1 Cor. 7. 29.

[41] Cf. Gen. 1. 28.

⁴² It is possible that Tertullian's views on the proximity of the *parousia* were influenced to some extent by a conviction that in his day the world's population had reached a saturation point. Men 'filled the earth,' the plan of God was realized, His command to 'increase and multiply' was fulfilled, and so the end had arrived. Tertullian certainly felt that the world was overpopulated. It is interesting to read in *De an.* 30. 4: 'The best argument (against metempsychosis) is to be found in the teeming population of the world. Our numbers are burdensome to the earth, which hardly has sufficient resources to sustain our life; our wants become more and more acute and we hear on all sides that nature is no longer able to supply our needs. Pestilence, famine, war, and earthquakes must be thought of as a remedy for this condition, a pruning, as it were, of the too fruitful race of men.' St. Jerome, writing of the problem of overpopulation in his day, says (*Adv. Helv.* 21): *iam plenus est orbis, terra nos non capit.*

⁴³ Matt. 3. 10.

⁴⁴ Ex. 21. 24; Lev. 24. 20; Deut. 19. 21; Matt. 5. 38. There is a lengthy explanation of the purpose of the *lex talionis* in *Adv. Marc.* 4. 16.

⁴⁵ Rom. 12. 17; 1 Thess. 5. 15; cf. Matt. 5. 39.

⁴⁶ The antithesis is expressed in the words *senuit* and *iuvenuit*.

⁴⁷ *Sacerdotes mei non plus nubent.* There is no such text in Leviticus. However, in Lev. 21. 7 priests are forbidden to marry harlots and divorcees, and in 21. 13 f. we read that the high priest 'shall take a virgin unto his wife; but a widow or one that is divorced or defiled or a harlot, he shall not take, but a maid of his own flesh.' Marriage is pluralized *ratione uxoris* if these prescriptions are not observed, and this is probably what Tertullian has in mind. It is worth noting that Ezechiel (44. 22) expressly permits priests to 'take a widow also, that is, the widow of a priest.'

⁴⁸ This is probably no more than a cryptic way of saying that marriage is one if it is contracted only once.

⁴⁹ Cf. Matt. 5. 17 f.

⁵⁰ Cf. Titus 1. 6. Here St. Paul writes 'priests' (πρεσβυτέρους), while in 1 Tim. 3. 2 he uses the word 'bishop' (ἐπίσκοπον). The terms are synonymous, however, in both these passages. Tertullian recognized a clear distinction between bishops and priests. They participate in the same sacerdotal power, but the bishop is the *summus sacerdos.* Cf. *Ad ux.* n. 65; d'Alès, *op. cit.* 219 f.

⁵¹ On the meaning of *bigamus* and *digamus* see TLL 2. 1983 and

5. 1115. *Bigamus* is the later word. It is usual now to speak of simultaneous polygamy as bigamy and successive polygamy as digamy. The distinction is not always observed, however, and in the Code of Canon Law, for example, the *bigami* who are impeded from the reception of Holy Orders by an irregularity *ex defectu* are those who *duo vel plura matrimonia valida successive contraxerunt* (c. 984. 4°). In *De monog.* 6, *digamus* (used of Abraham) indicates simultaneous polygamy; in *Ad ux.* 1. 7 and *De monog.* 12, it has reference to successive polygamy.

[52] The question of whether Tertullian was ever ordained a priest has been the subject of considerable discussion and it is still not settled. St. Jerome (*De vir. ill.* 53) speaks of him as *Tertullianus presbyter* and says that he lived as a priest of the Church until middle age, when he lapsed into Montanism. Still, the words of the present passage, *Nonne et laici sacerdotes sumus?* throw some doubt on the matter. For the literature, see O. Bardenhewer, *op. cit* 2. 379 and 381. To this may be added H. Koch, 'Nochmals — war Tertullian Priester?' *Theol. Stud. u. Krit.* 103 (1931) 108-114, and J. Klein, *Tertullian. Christliches Bewusstsein und sittliche Forderungen* (Abhandl. aus Ethik u. Moral 15, Düsseldorf 1940) 268-73.

[53] Apoc. 1. 6; compare *De monog.* 12. With his lapse into Montanism, Tertullian's views on the hierarchical constitution of the Church and on the priesthood of the laity became extremely unorthodox. The ecclesiology of this whole chapter is very bad. See the recent analysis in J. E. Rea, *The Common Priesthood of the Members of the Mystical Body* (Westminster, Md. 1947) esp. 10 f.; and P. Palmer, 'The Lay Priesthood: Real or Metaphorical?' *Theol. Stud.* 8 (1947) 574. Further material may be found in K. Adam, *Der Kirchenbegriff Tertullians. Eine dogmengeschichtliche Studie* (Forsch. z. christ. Lit.-u. Dogmengesch. 6. 4, Paderborn 1907); and G. Bardy, 'Le sacerdoce chrétien d'après Tertullien,' *La vie spirituelle* 58 Suppl. (1939) [109]-[124].

[54] *Differentiam inter ordinem et plebem constituit ecclesiae auctoritas*. . . . If the words *ecclesiae auctoritas* are taken in an active sense, they mean that the difference between clerics and lay persons is a human arrangement, made by the Church itself, and not the result of Christ's institution of a hierarchy. If taken passively, they mean that it is the possession of ecclesiastical authority which sets the clergy apart from the laity. The words which follow in the sentence suggest that the active sense is intended.

[55] The translation of this paragraph is based on Oehler's text. He reads here . . . *et honor per ordinis consessum sanctificatus. Adeo ubi.* . . . Kroymann's emendation reads . . . *per ordinis consessus sanctificatos deo. Ubi* . . . . The expression *ordinis consessus* means an assembly of those in orders, hence ' the hierarchy.' Palmer, *loc. cit.*, quotes *ordinis* . . . *concessus* as Oehler's reading in the following sentence. This is a misprint, but a suggestive one.

[56] *Adeo* often means *ideo* in Tertullian, and the sequence of thought seems to be this: ' Since, as has been said, it is merely an ecclesiastical distinction and not one of divine origin, therefore where there is . . . .' The words *ecclesiae auctoritas* are thus taken in an active sense. Cf. n. 54 above.

[57] Compare *De bap.* 6; *De orat.* 2, 28; *De pud.* 21; *De monog.* 7, 12. See d'Alès, *op. cit.* 492-94.

[58] Hab. 2. 4; Rom. 1. 17; Gal. 3. 11; Heb. 10. 38. In all of these passages it is the ' just man ' who is said to live by faith. Tertullian, however, wrote: *Unusquisque enim sua fide vivit.* . . .

[59] Cf. Rom. 2. 11 (2 Par. 19. 7, Wisd. 6. 8, Eph. 6. 9, Col. 3. 25) and 13 (Matt. 7. 21, 1 John 3. 7, James 1. 22, 25).

[60] Or, following Oehler, '. . . you must needs be living according to priestly discipline when an occasion arises which makes use of your sacerdotal powers a matter of necessity.' The various meanings of *disciplina* in the writings of Tertullian are discussed by V. Morel in his exhaustive study, ' *Disciplina*, le mot et l'idée représentée par lui dans les oeuvres de Tertullien,' *Rev. d'hist. ecclés.* 40 (1944/5) 5-46.

[61] The author uses the word *capitale*, ' capital sin.' A *capitale* was one of the unpardonable sins (*peccata irremissibilia* or *inconcessibilia*), of which there were seven in the listing of Tertullian (*Adv. Marc.* 4. 9): idolatry, blasphemy, homicide, adultery, fornication (*stuprum*), false witness, and fraud. A similar list is given in *De pud.* 19. 25. According to Tertullian, writing as a Montanist, such a sin — in the present argumentation he is evidently speaking of a second marriage as *stuprum* (cf. below, c. 9) — was irremissible in the sense that the Church could not effect forgiveness; penance, however, was not excluded, as the sinner might hope for forgiveness from God. Cf. B. Poschmann, *Paenitentia secunda. Die kirchliche Busse im ältesten Christentum bis Cyprian und Origenes* (Theophaneia 1, Bonn 1940) 283-348: ' Die Busslehre Tertullians '; d'Alès, *op. cit.* 272-75, 347, 479; C. Daly, ' The Sacrament of

Penance in Tertullian,' *Irish Ecclesiastical Record* 69 (1947) 693-707, 815-821; 70 (1948) 730-46, 832-48; 73 (1950) 156-69.

[62] There is an *a fortiori* argument here in an elliptical construction. Expressed completely, the argument would be: If it is a crime for a priest digamist to exercise sacerdotal functions (and it is, since such digamists are deposed from office), then it must be an even more serious crime for a digamist to do so who has not been officially appointed to exercise priestly powers. It is not clear, on Tertullian's principles, why this should be a more serious offense. For Tertullian's use of ellipsis, see Hoppe, *Syntax und Stil des Tertullian* 143-46, and the same author's *Beiträge zur Sprache und Kritik Tertullians* 43 ff.

[63] Cf. Eph. 4. 5.

[64] *Quam* here, as frequently, means *quam qui*. See E. Löfstedt, *Zur Sprache Tertullians* (Lunds Univ. Arsskr., N. F. Adv. 1. 16. 2, Lund-Leipzig 1920) 35.

[65] 1 Cor. 6. 12.

[66] Reading *utilitatis praestantiam sectetur*, Rigault's suggestion. For Tertullian's use of *praestantia* in the sense of *quod homines praestare possunt*, see Waszink, *op. cit.* 112. Cf. also F. Demmel, *Die Neubildungen auf -antia und -entia bei Tertullian* (diss. Zurich: Immensee 1944).

[67] Cf. 1 Cor. 9. 5. The Vulgate has *mulierem sororem*, Tertullian *uxores*; the Greek is ἀδελφὴν γυναῖκα. The word γυνή is ambiguous and can mean either ' woman ' or ' wife,' as Tertullian himself explains in *De monog.* 8, see n. 108. Tradition and context appear to exclude the view that St. Paul is speaking here of a wife, although there is no difficulty about admitting that he could have had one, if he had wished. He seems, rather, to be referring to Christian women who accompanied the Apostles in a ministerial capacity, after the example of those mentioned in Matt. 27. 55 and Luke 8. 1 ff. The interpretation, however, remains controversial. Cf. J. MacRory, *The Epistles of St. Paul to the Corinthians* (3rd ed. Dublin 1935) 124-26, and J. Huby, *Saint Paul: première épître aux Corinthiens* (Paris 1946) 204-206.

[68] Cf. *ibid.* 9. 14.

[69] St. Paul — cf. *ibid.* 9. 15.

[70] The word is *stuprum* (cf. above, n. 61). Athenagoras, *Suppl.* 33, had written some few years earlier that second marriage is little more than a ' decent way of committing adultery ' (εὐπρεπὴς μοιχεία).

[71] Cf. 1 Cor. 7. 32-34. The text has reference to the solicitude of both husband and wife, but Tertullian, in the sentences which fol-

low, emphasizes the solicitude of the wife to please her husband, although he retains 'they' as the subject.

[72] Matt. 5. 28. Tertullian here has *stupravit* for the Vulgate *moechatus est* (ἐμοίχευσεν). He cites this verse in many other passages, never using *stuprare*, but always a word clearly indicative of adultery: *De res. carn.* 15 (*adulteravit*); *De an.* 15. 4, 40. 4, 58. 6 (*adulteravit*); *De pud.* 6 (*moechatus est*); *De idol.* 2 (*adulterium designat*). For Tertullian's use of this verse, cf. G. J. D. Aalders, *Tertullianus' citaten uit de Evangeliën en de oud-Latijnsche Bijbelvertalingen* (diss. Amsterdam: 1932) 35.

[73] It is consent, not consummation, which constitutes the essence of marriage. Tertullian's statement here would seem to imply a belief in the so-called 'copula theory' of marriage. But contrast *De monog.* 10 and n. 145. For a refutation of this theory, see A. De Smet, *Betrothment and Marriage* (tr. from 3rd Latin ed. by W. Dobell, St. Louis 1923) 1. 59-65. An historical study may be found in A. Esmein, *Le mariage en droit canonique* (2nd ed. Paris 1929) 1. 101 ff.

[74] This is a perversion of the sense of Christ's words in Matt. 5. 28.

[75] *Inquit*, with no subject expressed. Kroymann supposes an adversary who had just objected that legal sanction for marriage differentiates it from adultery.

[76] This represents the lowest point in Tertullian's teaching on marriage. Not even in the *De monogamia* does he speak more disparagingly. His language as a Catholic was quite different. See the conclusion of *Ad uxorem*; also the Intro. to the present treatise, 41 and nn. 4, 5, and 6.

[77] 1 Cor. 7. 1. Tertullian has *optimum* ('best') for *bonum* ('good').

[78] *Modestia a modo intellegitur.*

[79] Repeated from *Ad ux.* 1. 5.

[80] Matt. 24. 19.

[81] Cf. 1 Cor. 7. 3.

[82] *Placet sibi*, that is, 'he takes pleasure in what he does'; or, possibly, 'he acts with a view to his own pleasure.'

[83] During the first two centuries of the Church all Christians acted as exorcists. The Fathers frequently assert that nothing more is needed to expel demons from persons, places, or things than to call on the name of Jesus, to recite simple prayers or verses from the Scriptures, or to make the Sign of the Cross. Cf. *Ad ux.* 2. 5 and n. 116; also J. Forget, 'Exorcisme,' DTC 5. 2 (1923) 1762-80. We do

not meet with a special order of exorcists in the Church until the third century. See J. Tixeront, *Holy Orders and Ordination* (tr. by S. A. Raemers, St. Louis 1928) 126 ff.

[84] Cf. 1 Cor. 7. 5.

[85] For Tertullian, the *spiritus* of a man is his life breath. The soul itself is called *spiritus*, not by reason of its substance, but by reason of this vital breath. Cf. *De anima*, especially 10 and 11, and Waszink, *op. cit.* 180 ff. In the present context *spiritus*, in the sense of life breath, is the soul as breathing prayer to God.

[86] Cf. Lev. 11. 44, 19. 2, 20. 7 and 1 Peter 1. 16. Tertullian quotes the text in the future indicative; in the Vulgate the future indicative is used in St. Peter, whereas the verses in Leviticus have the imperative, *sancti estote*.

[87] Psalm 17. 26 f.; cf. also 2 Kings 22. 26 f.

[88] Cf. Eph. 4. 1; Col. 1. 10; 1 Thess. 2. 12.

[89] Rom. 8. 6.

[90] The translation here is based on de Labriolle's careful analysis of the passage in *La crise montaniste* (Paris 1913) 77-84. The initial words are especially difficult: *Purificantia enim concordat.* F. Leitner, 'Die Biblische Inspiration,' *Bibl. Studien* 1 (1896) 118 n. 3, interpreted them as meaning that purity effects a mystical union with God; de Labriolle (83) suggests that they mean: purity diffuses harmony into the souls of such as wish to pray. The Montanists, especially the two women Prisca (or Priscilla) and Maximilla (cf. de Labriolle 23-31) claimed to have received a divine *afflatus*, identified with the Paraclete, inspiring them to preach the new prophecy in preparation for the imminent coming of the new Jerusalem. Their 'revelations' have been partially preserved in some nineteen oracles. See de Labriolle 34-105, and A. Harnack, *History of Dogma* (tr. from the 3rd German ed. by N. Buchanan, London 1896) 2. 95 ff. The present quotation from Prisca is found only in the *Codex Agobardinus*. A pious scruple, as de Labriolle observes (77), kept it out of the other remaining manuscripts, thus accounting also for its absence in the early editions of Tertullian.

[91] Tertullian's language in this chapter raises the important question of his belief in the existence of Purgatory. The principle passages from his works which are cited in support of the view that he held this doctrine are: *De an.* 35. 1, 58. 8; *De res. carn.* 42; *Adv. Marc.* 3. 24, 5. 10. It is clear from a synthesis of these passages that Tertullian believed in the existence of a prison house where, after death, separated souls destined ultimately for beatitude but

still capable of suffering, are detained for a longer or shorter time according to their merits, until they 'pay the last farthing' (Matt. 5. 26) of the debt which they have contracted by their sins. Moreover, prayers are said for the souls of those who have passed away (cf. the present passage), and this is done in order to obtain for them a tempering or alleviation of some sort of suffering (*refrigerium*) and a share in the 'first resurrection' (*De monog.* 10). This, of course, is not a complete description of what we now call Purgatory, but it does contain almost all of the essential features found in the doctrine as it is proposed today. R. Roberts, *op. cit.* 208, says this is 'the germ from which the later theory of Purgatory developed'; and Harnack, *History of Dogma* 2. 296, declares: 'The idea of a kind of Purgatory — a notion which does not originate with the realistic but with the philosophic eschatology — is quite plainly found in Tertullian.'

It may be admitted that Tertullian's views on this subject are badly tainted by his chiliastic eschatology, as, for example, in the distinction which he makes between the first and second resurrection. It may also be admitted that he nowhere asserts that the *interim* sufferings of souls which will enjoy final blessedness, are positive purgatorial pains. In a crucial passage (*De an.* 58. 8), however, he does say that such souls are detained in a 'prison house,' and he interprets the 'payment of the last farthing' as the penalty which is exacted for even the slightest transgression (*modicum quoque debitum illic luendum*). This penalty, he says, consists in the postponement of the resurrection, and he concludes that 'therefore there can be no doubt that already during the *interim* the soul receives retribution for its deeds' (*aliquid pensare penes inferos*). Of this passage d'Alès asks, *op. cit.* 134 f. n. 2: 'Qu'est-ce que cette attente douloureuse, sinon un purgatoire?'

A. J. Mason, 'Tertullian and Purgatory,' *Jour. of Theol. Stud.* 3 (1902) 598-601, feels that Tertullian's failure to mention the existence of positive purgatorial pains makes it impossible to argue from this passage to his belief in the existence of a purgatory where the soul is cleansed by suffering. However, 'purgatorial suffering' actually means no more than suffering which removes a debt, the *reatus poenae temporalis*, contracted by sin (*poena piacularis*). Tertullian's language in *De an.* 58. 8 certainly shows that the removal of a debt is effected by the exaction of a penalty which consists in the *mora resurrectionis*. Thus his description is remarkably consistent with what theologians, in describing the punishment of Purgatory, call *satispassio,* a term used to indicate that by suffering *poenae pure vindictivae* the souls in Purgatory are freed from the temporal punishment which is due their sins. See L. Lercher, *Institutiones theologiae dogmaticae* (3rd ed. Innsbruck 1949) 4. 2. 456-65. There is no ecclesiastical definition concerning the nature of the punishment suffered in Purgatory, but theologians are agreed that it consists in a *poena damni,* which is the deferment of the beatific vision, and a *poena sensus,* which is some sort of positive, externally inflicted suffering. Tertullian's description of Purgatory is defective because he fails to state that the pain of Purgatory is positive; it is not defective because he fails to use the word 'purgatorial.' The positive pain of Purgatory, the *poena sensus,* is described quite vividly in later writers; cf. the sufferings of Dinocrates related in the *Pass. SS. Perp. et Fel.* 2, on which see F. J. Dölger, AC 2 (1930) 1-40. For the literature on this whole question, cf. Waszink, *op. cit.* 591-93.

⁹² The clause reads . . . *pro qua oblationes annuas reddis. Oblatio* can mean the offering of the Eucharist, that is, the Mass itself, or the gifts which the faithful offer when Mass is celebrated. See also Tertullian, *De virg. vel.* 9; *De cor.* 3; *De monog.* 10; *Ad ux.* 2. 8, and above, ch. 7 of the present treatise. That as early as approximately 170 A. D. the Eucharistic sacrifice was offered for the dead on the third day following burial and, most probably also on the anniversary days — as is here supported by Tertullian — has been shown by F. J. Dölger, ΙΧΘΥΣ (2nd ed. Münster i. W. 1928) 555-69: 'Die Totenmesse.'

⁹³ The prayer is for gifts *bonae mentis* (*inter cetera bonae mentis* is Oehler's conjecture), that is to say, gifts which are proper to an upright soul. *Mens,* by metonymy, is a synonym for *anima,* since *mens* (or *animus,* the Greek νοῦς) is that property of the soul by which it acts and thinks (*quo agit, quo sapit*): *De an.* 12. 1. Kroymann, however, understands *bonae mentis* as referring to the wife's disposition: 'If she is well disposed, will you ask for the gift of chastity in your prayers?'

⁹⁴ Compare this chapter with *Ad ux.* 1. 4 f.

⁹⁵ Cf. 2 Tim. 2. 3 f.: '*Labora sicut bonus miles Christi Iesu.*' The concept of life on earth as a combat, a soldiering for God, is also found in the Old Testament; e. g. Job 7. 1: '*Militia est vita hominis super terram.*' The early Christian writers draw constantly on the language of the military profession to describe the Christian's labors for God and Heaven, and his struggles wtih the world and the devil. Cf. the study by A. Harnack, *Militia Christi. Die christliche*

Religion und der Soldatenstand in den ersten drei Jahrhunderten
(Tübingen 1905). Persecution and martyrdom, monasticism and
asceticism, were especially provocative of military allusions and terminology. Cf. E. L. Hummel, *The Concept of Martyrdom according to St. Cyprian of Carthage* (SCA 9, Washington 1950) 56-90:
'Martyrdom as a Spiritual Warfare'; E. E. Malone, *The Monk and
the Martyr* (SCA 12, Washington 1950) 91-111: 'Martyrdom and
Monastic Life as a "militia spiritualis."' Cf. also ACW 2. 148 n.
148; 5. 190 n. 140; 7. 303 n. 191.

[96] Cf. 2 Cor. 5. 6; Heb. 11. 13; and Tertullian, *De res. carn.* 43.

[97] Cf. below, *De monog.*, n. 198.

[98] With reference to the injunction in the Sermon on the Mount,
Matt. 6. 34: '*Nolite ergo soliciti esse in crastinum.*'

[99] Cf. Phil. 1. 23.

[100] The words are . . . qui illi *parentent*. Tertullian sarcastically
supposes that the children of a Christian digamist follow a pagan
ritual when they honor him at his grave. Of the several occasions
on which the Romans commemorated their dead, the *Parentalia* were
the most popular and most widespread. This commemorative season,
during which the public officials put off the *toga praetexta*, temples
were closed, and no weddings were allowed, extended from February
13th to the 21st. The first eight days were reserved for private cult
of the family dead — the *di parentum* — when their tombs were
decorated and they were offered sacrifices of wine, milk, honey, etc.
The ninth day was given over to a public honoring of the dead (cf.
Ovid, *Fast.* 2. 533-616). The verb used to describe this honoring
of the dead is *parentare*, the action is *parentatio*; both Kellner and
Thelwall are obviously in error when they associate *parentare* with
funeral rites. Elsewhere Tertullian severely criticizes and derides
the pagan *parentatio*: see the beginning of his *De resurrectione
carnis*. St. Augustine contrasts the pagan and Christian practices,
indicating also a reversion to the pagan ritual by some Christians,
in *De civ. Dei* 8. 27. On the *parentalia*, cf. G. Wissowa, *Religion
und Kultus der Römer* (2nd ed. Munich 1912) 232 f.; on pagan and
Christian funeral and burial rites, A. C. Rush, *Death and Burial in
Christian Antiquity* (SCA 1, Washington 1941) 187-273.

[101] *Christianis leonem*: in the more familiar form, *Apol.* 40. 1:
Christianos ad leonem! Cf. also *Mart. Polycarpi* 12. 2; Cyprian,
Epist. 59. 6.

[102] Compare *Ad ux.* 1. 5.

[103] The procurement of abortion by means of drugs is frequently

mentioned and condemned by ancient Christian writers and early Church councils. Minucius Felix, *Oct.* 30. 2, speaks of pagans who kill their children yet unborn *medicaminibus epotis*, and St. Jerome *Epist.* 22. 13, states that there are Christian women (*Christi adulterae*) who conceive illegitimately and then use poison to procure an abortion. Frequently this causes their own death and they go down to hell guilty of three crimes: suicide, adultery, and murder. Numerous other references in ancient writers to the use of abortifacients are given by Oehler 1. 147 and J. H. Waszink, 'Abtreibung,' RAC 1 (1950) 55-60.

Uncertainty as to the exact time when the foetus began to lead an independent, human life was responsible for some variation among the ancients in judging the morality of abortion. It may be said, in general, that even among the pagans, abortion was looked upon as murder when the foetus was considered as having its own proper, individual life. For a comparative study of Christian and pagan views on the subject of abortion, see Waszink, *ibid.*, and F. J. Dölger's articles referred to above, n. 45 *Ad ux.*

[104] Cf. Gen. 18. 10-14, 21. 1 f. (Sara, wife of Abraham); 1 Kings 1. 1-20 (Anna, wife of Elcana); Luke 1 (Elizabeth, wife of Zachary).

[105] The *pronuba* was the woman who attended the bride throughout the marriage ceremony. That she had to be a monogamist is also stated elsewhere; e. g. Festus p. 4. 349 Lindsay: '*Pronubae adhibebantur nuptis, quae semel nupserunt, ut matrimonii perpetuitatem auspicantes.*' Cf. also Paulus, *ibid*; the same is reported on the authority of Varro by Servius in his note to Virgil, *Aen.* 4. 166 (1. 493. 3 f. Thilo-Hagen): '*Varro pronubam dicit quae ante nupsit et quae uni tantum nupta est.*' On the duties of the *pronuba*, cf. J. Carcopino, *Daily Life in Ancient Rome* (tr. from the French by E. O. Lorimer, New Haven 1940); A. E. Paoli, *Das Leben im alten Rom* (Bern 1948) 148.

[106] This is emphasized by Paulus (4. 349 Lindsay), who states that a *pronuba* was chosen who had married only once as an augury of the unity of the marriage about to be contracted: '*pronubae adhibebantur nuptis, quae semel nupserunt, causa auspicii, ut singulare perseveraret matrimonium.*

[107] Compare the illustrations of this chapter with those in *Ad ux.* 1. 6 and *De monog.* 17. — The *Flamines* were priests of Rome dedicated to the special service of some particular deity. There were three of major and three of minor rank. The principal *Flamen* was the *Flamen Dialis* (of Jupiter). His wife, the *Flaminica*, was

priestess of Juno. She had to be *univira*, 'of one husband,' and her consort could not divorce her: cf. Wissowa, *op. cit.* 506 n. 4. It is to these two that Tertullian has reference. Cf. also H. J. Rose, 'Flamines,' OCD 364.

[108] See above, *Ad ux.* n. 69 and Wissowa, *op. cit.* 508 ff.

[109] Cf. H. J. Rose, 'Vesta, Vestals,' OCD 943 f. Plutarch, *Numa* 10, states that in historical times, the Vestal Virgins served for thirty years and during this time were obligated to remain virgins, but were free to marry when their term had expired. See above, *Ad ux.* n. 56.

[110] Cf. *Ad ux.* n. 58.

[111] Probably Apis, or Hapi, the bull god worshiped at Memphis. Cf. R. Pietschmann, 'Apis' no. 4, RE 1 (1884) 2807-9.

[112] *Aliqua Dido.* *Aliquis*, placed before well-known proper names, is an oddity of Tertullian's style. Cf. Hoppe, *Syntax u. Stil d. Tert.* 105.

[113] Virgil's account in the *Aeneid* of the death of Dido is a late variation of the story. According to the earlier account, Elissa, a daughter of the king of Tyre (called Dido after the Phoenician goddess of the moon), fled to Africa to escape her brother Pygmalion, who had murdered her husband. To avoid marriage with Iarbas, a barbarian king, she erected a funeral pyre and committed suicide by stabbing herself upon it. Cf. R. Heinze, *Virgils epische Technik* (4th ed. Leipzig 1928) 114 f. It is this version of the story that Tertullian prefers. Compare *Apol.* 50. 3 (where also — cf. note immediately preceding: *aliqua Carthaginis conditrix*) and *Ad mart.* 4.

[114] Lucretia, the wife of Collatinus, was dishonored by Sextus Tarquinius. Her suicide led to the expulsion of the Tarquins from Rome. The story is told in Livy 1. 58 f.; Dionysius of Halicarnassus 4. 64 ff.

[115] *Ordo* is frequently used in the sense of ecclesiastical 'estate.' Widows and virgins belonged to such an 'order' or 'estate' but they were not ordained in the sense in which we understand the word today. Cf. J. Tixeront, *Holy Orders and Ordination* 297; also above, *Ad ux.* n. 66.

[116] Apparently, the honor lost by their first marriage.

[117] 'Paradise' as a synonym for 'Heaven' recurs constantly in the ancient inscriptions for the Christian dead; Cf. C. Mohrmann, *Die altchristliche Sondersprache in den Sermones des hl. Augustin* (Lat. christ. primaeva 3, Nijmegen 1932) 132. The usage is familiar to us from the antiphon sung at the grave: '*In Paradisum* deducant te angeli. . . .'

¹¹⁸ Cf. Matt. 22. 30; Mark 12. 25; Luke 20. 35. — In one of the Florentine codices the treatise ends with the wish that 'grace may be with him who accepts this'; and with the plea, 'in your prayers remember Tertullian, who exhorts you to do so.' Cf. the concluding words of the *De baptismo*.

MONOGAMY

INTRODUCTION

[1] The quotations in this paragraph are all taken from ch. 1. Other, more specific accusations are found in later chapters; they include a vicious attack on the private life of one of the Catholic bishops (12).

[2] See, for example, 2: *Mongamiae disciplinam in haeresim expro-bant.* Also, 15: *Quae haeresis, si secundas nuptias, ut illicitas, iuxta adulterium iudicamus?* This point is further discussed by A. Hauck, *Tertullian's Leben und Schriften* (Erlangen 1877) 397; de Labriolle, *La crise montaniste*, 383.

[3] Cf. 10 and 11. In the *Ad uxorem* and the *De exhortatione castitatis* Tertullian neglected to answer adequately the serious diffi-culty against his position found in 1 Cor. 7. 39: 'A woman is bound as long as her husband is alive, but, if her husband dies, she is free. Let her marry whom she pleases . . . .' It was this text, apparently, which his adversaries quoted against him, and he studies it at great length in the present treatise.

[4] E. Rolffs, *Urkunden aus dem antimontanistischen Kampfe des Abendlandes* (*Texte und Unters.* 12. 4, Leipzig 1895) 50-109.

[5] Harnack, *Die Chronologie der altchrist. Litt.* 2. 287, is in sym-pathy with Rolffs' theory, but he admits that it cannot be proved. It is opposed by Bardenhewer, *op. cit.* 2. 422, de Labriolle, *op. cit.* 383, and Monceaux, *op. cit.* 428.

[6] St. Jerome writes (*De vir. ill.* 53) that Tertullian became a Montanist because of the 'envy and insults of the Roman clergy' and adds that after his lapse he composed a number of treatises in which he dealt with the new prophecy — *specialiter autem adversus Ecclesiam texuit volumina de pudicitia, de persecutione, de ieiuniis, de monogamia, de exstasi.* It is impossible to say just how well organ-ized Montanism was at Carthage before Tertullian gave his support to the movement.

[7] In the first chapter of the *De ieiunio* Tertullian speaks of a work of his 'already composed in defense of monogamy.'

⁸ There are frequent references in the *De pudicitia* to the illegitimacy of second marriage. The whole treatise should be read in conjunction with the *De monogamia* to obtain a complete picture of Tertullian's views on the subject.

⁹ Ch. 3.

¹⁰ De Labriolle, *op. cit.* 392, says of the *De monogamia*: 'Jamais Tertullien n'a été aussi vif, aussi nerveux, aussi pressant que dans cet ouvrage.'

¹¹ Tertullian's personality and its influence on the great decisions of his life has been the subject of a recent analysis by B. Nisters, *Tertullian: Seine Persönlichkeit und sein Schicksal* (Münster i. W. 1950). On Tertullian's place in the rigorist movement of his age, and on rigorism as a persistent phenomenon in Church history, see R. Knox, *Enthusiasm* (Oxford 1950), especially 25-49. For estimates of Tertullian's character which are more favorable than those usually encountered, cf. the excellent paper by J. Tixeront, 'Tertullien moraliste,' *Mélanges de patrologie et d'histoire des dogmes* (2nd ed. Paris 1921) 117-152; and C. De Lisle Shortt, *The Influence of Philosophy on the Mind of Tertullian* (London n. d.) 98-105.

TEXT

¹ Tertullian is probably referring to the Marcionite rejection of marriage. Cf. *Ad uxorem* n. 15, and *Adv. Marc.* 5. 7.

² In his Montanist writings Tertullian habitually uses the epithet 'Sensualists' or 'Psychics' in speaking of Catholics. The word *psychicus* is derived from St. Paul's ἄνθρωπος ψυχικός (1 Cor. 2. 14), i. e. the carnal or animal man as opposed to the spiritual, the ἄνθρωπος πνευματικός. See the careful explanation of these terms and their use by the Montanists in de Labriolle's *La crise montaniste* 138-43; cf. also E. Evans, *Tertullian's Treatise against Praxeas* (SPCK, London 1948) 81, 187 f.

³ The word is *ingerunt* — cf. Hoppe, *Syntax u. Stil. d. Tert.* 133.

⁴ The opposition here is between *alienos spadones* and *aurigas tuos*, literally, 'heretical eunuchs and your charioteers,' that is, those Catholics who race on to excesses. The words show that Tertullian still considers his opponents to be members of the true Church of Christ. His position resembles rather closely that of the Jansenists; he wished to lead a movement for what he considered reform within the Church and had no desire to depart from it, or to split its unity. His great error on the subject of marriage is to prefer

the hysterical utterances of Montanus and his prophetesses to the clear and sober teaching of St. Paul.

⁵ Or 'would make a caricature of Him' (*confundit*).

⁶ Gal. 5. 17. The word 'spirit' (πνεῦμα) in St. Paul means a) the soul of a man as the principle of thought or consciousness; b) the activity of the Holy Spirit; c) the person of the Holy Spirit. In about half the places where St. Paul uses the word it is impossible to say which of these meanings he intends. Cf. Prat, *op. cit.* 2. 405. Tertullian takes any sense from the text of St. Paul which he finds best suited to his argument at the time.

⁷ Gen. 6. 3.

⁸ Montanism was a Pneumocentric system. A fundamental tenet of its adherents was that the 'new prophecy' came to them as a revelation of the Paraclete. Some Montanists distinguished the Paraclete from the Holy Spirit, asserting that the Holy Spirit had descended upon the Apostles, while the reception of the Paraclete was reserved for the saints of their own day. As is evident from the present chapter of this treatise, Tertullian made no such distinction. See R. B. Hoyle, 'The Paraclete in Tertullian's Writings,' *Bibl. Rev.* 16 (1931) 170-89.

⁹ Cf. Matt. 11. 30.

¹⁰ John 16. 12, *Cum autem venerit ille Spiritus veritatis docebit* . . . . Tertullian has, . . . *cum venerit spiritus sanctus, ille vos ducet in omnem veritatem.* Cf. also John 14. 26.

¹¹ Cf. John 16. 13 f.

¹² Cf. Rom. 6. 19.

¹³ Cf. Matt. 19. 12.

¹⁴ The text has:. . . *ipso Domino spadonibus aperiente regna caelorum, ut et ipso spadone, ad quem spectans et Apostolus propterea et ipse castratus continentiam mavult.*

¹⁵ Cf. 1 Cor. 7. 1, quoted two sentences farther on.

¹⁶ Tertullian is unable or unwilling to make a distinction between 'the good' and 'the better.' St. Paul is obviously speaking of 'good' in a relative, not an absolute sense. See above, *De exhort. cast.* 3 and n. 24 to the same treatise.

¹⁷ 1 Cor. 7. 29.

¹⁸ Cf. *ibid.* 7. 32 ff.

¹⁹ *Ibid.* 7. 7.

²⁰ *Ibid.* 7. 9.

²¹ The last two paragraphs are taken almost verbatim from *De exhort. cast.* 3.

²² 1 Cor. 7. 10.

²³ *Ibid.* a conflation of 7. 7 and 40.

²⁴ Cf. 1 John 2. 6.

²⁵ *Ibid.* 3. 3.

²⁶ An adaptation of 1 Peter 1. 16. Cf. above, n. 86 to *De exhort. cast.* Tertullian, as is evident from what follows and from the use of the past tense (*fuit*) understands the text as referring to the sanctity of Christ.

²⁷ Sanctity here has reference to sexual purity. The *spiritus* in question is not the Holy Spirit, as Thelwall supposes, but rather man's spirit or soul, as opposed to his body.

²⁸ That is, the same Holy Spirit who inspired the Apostles when they wrote the texts just quoted.

²⁹ Cf. John 15. 13.

³⁰ Cf. Eccles. 3. 1, 17.

³¹ Cf. 1 Cor. 7. 29.

³² The First Epistle to the Corinthians was written about 57 A. D. See the Intro. (68) above.

³³ The sentence reads: *In hoc quoque paracletum agnoscere debes advocatum, quod a tota continentia infirmitatem tuam excusat.* A 'paraclete' (παρακαλέω), literally, is one who is called to the aid of another. Hence, in numerous passages the Latin Fathers have *advocatus* for *paraclitus* of the Vulgate. After the fourth century it became more common to explain the word as meaning *consolator.* Cf. P. Ceuppens, *Theologia Biblica* (2nd ed. Rome 1949) 2. 265 f. St. Augustine (*Tract. in Ioan.* 94. 2) says that both meanings are acceptable: '*Consolator ergo ille vel advocatus (utrumque enim interpretatur quod est graece paracletus) Christo abscedente fuerat necessarius.*' For παράκλητος in the sense of an advocate in court, cf. Liddell-Scott-Jones; the usage appears to have been frequent in the rabbinic literature and references may be found in Ceuppens, *loc. cit.*

³⁴ *Evolvamus communia instrumenta scripturarum pristinarum.* Tertullian's training in the law leads him to speak of the Scriptures as *instrumenta*, that is, records having a legal value. They are documents which, as it were, confer legal rights on the doctrine which they contain. The words *communia instrumenta* are but one instance of many which might be cited to show that he recognized the existence of a definite canon, comprising books of both the Old and the New Testament. Cf. d'Alès, *op. cit.* 223-30. The docu-

ments are *communia* because accepted by both Catholics and Montanists alike.

[35] Gen. 2. 18.

[36] *Ibid.* 2. 24. Cf. above, n. 32 to *De exhort. cast.*

[37] Of course, it makes a great deal of difference whether polygamy is simultaneous or successive. Tertullian is guilty of a childish literalism when he argues that if a man has two wives, even though one is divorced or dead, he still has two wives. He is correct in saying (11) that divorce does not dissolve the marriage bond. Christ says the same (Mark 10. 11 f.; Luke 16. 18). He errs when he says that not even death dissolves it. St. Paul says that it does (Rom. 7. 2 f.; 1 Cor. 7. 39).

[38] The men who lived before the flood.

[39] Since Scripture says nothing about the practice of polygamy before the flood, it denies that it then existed. In the *De corona* (2), written just a few years before the composition of the present work, Tertullian had said that a thing is prohibited if it is not positively permitted, and in the *De exhortatione castitatis* (4) he asserts that if St. Paul had wished second marriage, he would have explicitly commanded it. Such abuses of the argument from silence are frequent in his writings.

[40] Cf. Gen. 4. 24, where Lamech says to his wives: ' Sevenfold vengeance shall be taken for Cain; but for Lamech, seventy times sevenfold.' The verse has nothing to do with a punishment deserved for bigamy.

[41] *Reformari* is often equivalent to *renasci* in Tertullian (cf. Waszink, *op. cit.* 387 f.); so, too, beginning with Tertullian, *censeri = oriri* (cf. Waszink 282).

[42] Gen. 7. 7. reads ' the *wives* of his sons,' which is not conclusive. St. Peter, however, writing on the efficacy of baptism, says that ' when the ark was a building, . . . eight souls were saved by water' (1 Peter 3. 20). Tertullian's failure to quote from this epistle in the present context is not ascribable to ignorance of its existence, since he cites it elsewhere: *Scorp.* 12 (1 Peter 2. 20; 4. 12); *ibid.* 14 (1 Peter 2. 13); *De orat.* 20 (1 Peter 3. 3); cf. H. Rönsch, *Das Neue Testament Tertullians* (Leipzig 1871) 558.

[43] For this and other meanings of *recognoscere*, cf. G. F. Diercks, *Q. Septimius Florens Tertullianus: De oratione* (diss. Amsterdam: Bussum 1947) 76 f.

[44] Gen. 6. 19.

[45] Cf. Gen. 7. 2 f., ' Seven and seven, male and female' are to

be selected. That they were paired off with any kind of even relative permanence is an assumption of Tertullian's.

[46] Reading, with Oehler, *Quae utique lex est, non monimentum*; supposing *monimentum*, the sentence might also be translated, 'it is not merely a memory.' The MSS have *non nomine tunc* and Kellner, *suo nomine tunc*.

[47] Matt. 19. 8.

[48] *Ibid.* 19. 6.

[49] Eph. 1. 9 f.

[50] Cf. Apoc. 1. 8: 'I am Alpha and Omega, the beginning and the end, saith the Lord God.' Cf. *ibid.* 21. 6 and 22. 13. This device, illustrating that God and Christ are without beginning and end, is employed by other early Christian writers (Prudentius, *Cath.* 9. 10-12; Jerome, *Adv. Iovin.* 1. 18; etc.), and is also found in inscriptions and early Christian art: cf. F. Cabrol, ' AΩ,' DACL 1. 1 (1907) 1-25.

[51] Cf. John 1. 1.-14.

[52] The covenant of circumcision was not established until after the call of Abraham. See Gen. 17. In the first council of Jerusalem it was decided that the rite was not to be imposed upon converts to Christianity. See Acts 15.

[53] Cf. Gen. 9. 3 f. and Acts 15. 29.

[54] That is, the perfection of virginity; see below, n. 56. This sentence is susceptible of various interpretations, none of which is completely satisfactory.

[55] The words may also be translated 'demand that that which was from the beginning should be as it was in the beginning.'

[56] Tertullian forgets or ignores the fact that Adam was married before the fall. Cf. Gen. 1. 27 f.; 2. 22-25. See below, n. 214.

[57] Cf. Eph. 5. 32. The words of Genesis quoted by St. Paul are not restricted to the union of Adam and Eve, as Tertullian implies, but refer to marriage in general.

[58] Retaining *competentes* of the MSS for *competisse* (Rigault-Oehler); cf. Dr. Plumpe's remarks: 'Some Recommendations Regarding the Text of Tertullian's *De Monogamia*,' *Theol. Studies* 12 (Dec. 1951).

[59] The sense is: Now that you have once married you ought to practice monogamy according to the example He gives you in the spirit. Though, of course, before your marriage you had the obligation of following the higher ideal of perfect virginity which He gave you in the flesh.

[60] Cf. Matt. 23. 9.

[61] 1 Cor. 4. 15.

[62] Gal. 3. 7.

[63] Gen. 15. 6, quoted by St. Paul in Rom. 4. 3 and Gal. 3. 6.

[64] Cf. Rom. 4. 10 f., where St. Paul states that faith was 'reputed to him unto justice' when he was still 'in uncircumcision.'

[65] Cf. Gen. 17. 10-14.

[66] Tertullian's efforts to connect Abraham's uncircumcision with the practice of monogamy are not happy. His error in the present sentence seems inexplicable, since we read that 'Abraham was fourscore and six years old when Agar brought him forth Ismael' (Gen. 16. 16) and that it was only 'after he began to be ninety and nine' (Gen. 17. 1) that he received the covenant of circumcision. It is possible that inaccuracies such as these are the result of quoting from memory.

[67] This is an echo of Rom. 4. 11. Paul writes that Abraham received circumcision as a *signaculum iustitiae quae est in praeputio*. By this he means that Abraham, while still uncircumcised, was justified by faith and thereupon received circumcision as a seal of his justification. Tertullian has . . . *ex signaculo fidei in praeputiatione iustificatae*. The expression is not too clear, though the context shows that he merely wishes to oppose circumcision to faith as he opposes bigamy to monogamy.

[68] Cf. Gal. 3 and 4.

[69] Cf. Gen. 17. 5.

[70] *Exinde res viderint*. This, with the preceding sentence, probably means that when Abraham fell into the practice of polygamy he lost the authority of a father in our regard. Thereafter the question of the legitimacy or illegitimacy of multiple marriages is to be decided on its own merits and not by his example. Oehler's note (1. 450) on *De cor.* 13 illustrates Tertullian's fondness for this use of *viderint*.

[71] *Forma* is used here in the sense of a law or norm. On the various meanings of this word in Tertullian see Evans, *op. cit.*, 54 f. In legal terminology *forma* is a statute or custom to which a lawyer appeals in pleading a case. — For the meaning of *figura* in Tertullian, see Evans, *op. cit.* 321. The use of the word in the present passage of the *De monogamia* has been cited in support of the view that Tertullian held for a mere figurative presence of Christ in the Eucharist; cf. H. B. Swete, 'Eucharistic Belief in the Second and Third Centuries,' *Jour. of Theol. Studies* 3 (1902) 173. For a more

complete study of this question see Rauschen, *op. cit.* 11-14 and the literature there listed.

⁷² Cf. Gal. 4. 24.

⁷³ Cf. *ibid.* 4. 28.

⁷⁴ The twelve sons of Jacob were born of four different women: Gen. 35. 22-26.

⁷⁵ Cf. Num. 12. 8; Deut. 34. 10; Exod. 33. 11.

⁷⁶ The expression *populus secundus* has reference to a second 'generation' of the people. The *populus primus* was the generation which God punished by exclusion from the promised land. Cf. Num. 14 and Deut. 1. 35-39.

⁷⁷ 'Prototype,' i. e. the Jews. Their leader's name, Josue ('Jahweh saves'), was written 'Jesus' in the Septuagint; see also in the New Testament: Acts 7. 45; Heb. 4. 8. On Tertullian's principle that 'what Scripture does not assert it denies,' one might argue that Josue was not married at all, since there is no mention anywhere of his wife or children.

⁷⁸ *Paratura*, lit. 'preparation,' 'material,' 'apparatus,' etc., a word much favored by Tertullian (cf. Oehler's note, 1. 24 f., to *De spect.* 4), is frequently used by him in referring to Scripture (cf. Waszink, *op. cit.* 105).

⁷⁹ Cf. Matt. 5. 17.

⁸⁰ Cf. Basil, *Epist.* 160. 3.

⁸¹ Cf. Acts 15. 10 — St. Peter speaking before the council of Apostles and elders at Jerusalem. Tertullian says that this sentiment is *secundum sententiam apostolorum.*

⁸² Matt. 5. 20.

⁸³ Deut. 25. 5. This is the so-called law of the levirate. Theories on the origin and purpose of this law are discussed in E. Neufeld, *Ancient Hebrew Marriage Laws* (London 1944) 25-33.

⁸⁴ Cf. Matt. 22. 23 ff.; Mark 12. 18 ff.; Luke 20. 27 f. The question raised here was not entirely academic since there is some evidence that the law of the levirate was still observed at the time of Christ.

⁸⁵ Cf. Exod. 20. 5. The text has reference to the protracted evil effects of sin. It is intended as a statement of fact, not as the enunciation of a law, and it is as valid for the New Testament as for the Old.

⁸⁶ 1 Cor. 7. 29. See *De exhort. cast.* 6.

⁸⁷ Jer. 31. 29 f. See also Ezech. 18. 2.

⁸⁸ Cf. Matt. 19. 12.

[89] It is possible to see here an early reference to the ecclesiastical impediment of affinity. Classic Roman law declared affinity in the direct line an impediment to marriage, but the civil impediment was not extended to the collateral line until after the accession of the Christian emperors. Cf. W. W. Buckland, *op. cit.* 116. The first record of the canonical impediment is found in the Council of Elvira (about 300 A. D.) which excommunicates those who marry a deceased wife's sister (canon 61). St. Basil, however, in a letter addressed to Diodorus of Tarsus (*Epist.* 162. 2), says that according to an *immemorial tradition* such marriages have been considered by holy men as null and void. For a history of the impediment, see Joyce, *op. cit.* 534 ff.

[90] Cf. Matt. 23. 8.

[91] Cf. 1 Cor. 7. 39.

[92] Nationality was not an impediment to marriage among the Hebrews. Exogamy was widely practiced and there are no sanctions in the Bible against it. It appears to be the implication of Deut. 23. 4, however, that marriage with the Moabites and Ammonites was forbidden. A general disapproval of mixed marriage on religious grounds is expressed often enough. Cf. Exod. 34. 16; Deut. 7. 3; 3 Kings 11. 1; 2 Esd. 13. 23 ff.

[93] Lev. 20. 21, freely quoted. This is an apparent exception to the law of the levirate. Possibly the prohibition here has reference to a marriage with a brother's wife when the brother is still living; but see Neufeld, *op. cit.* 43 ff., for other solutions.

[94] The argument leads to an absolute prohibition of marriage for all widows and appears to make St. Paul's exception meaningless: she may marry again provided she marries someone whom she is forbidden to marry! Tertullian's attempt to explain away St. Paul's teaching on second marriage is found in chapters 10-14 of the present treatise.

[95] There is no such law. Lev. 21. 14, which d'Alès (*op. cit.* 471) thinks Tertullian refers to, prohibits the High Priest from marrying a widow or divorcee. The Talmud and later rabbinic literature, however, interpret the text as requiring the High Priest to be monogamous.

[96] Lev. 22. 13. The text grants a permission; it does not contain a command. The passage in which it occurs has to do with legislation regarding persons who may or may not eat the food offered in the sanctuary.

[97] Exod. 20. 12.

[98] The modern literature on baptism as 'putting on Christ' is listed by Waszink, *op. cit.* 520 f. To it may be added Prat's note (*op. cit.* 2. 462-66) on 'baptism in Christ,' and 'baptism in the name of Christ.' See also E. J. Duncan, *Baptism in the Demonstrations of Aphraates the Persion Sage* (SCA 8, Washington 1945) 43-49: 'Baptism as the Garment of Immortality.'

[99] Apoc. 1. 6. Baptism as the sacrament of initiation into the lay priesthood is discussed by L. Audet, *Notre participation au sacerdoce du Christ* (Quebec 1938) 50 ff.; see also P. Dabin, *Le sacerdoce royal des fidèles dans la tradition ancienne et moderne* (Brussels 1950). A more complete statement of Tertullian's views on the priesthood of the laity may be found in *De exhort. cast.* 7.

[100] Cf. Matt. 8. 21; Luke 9. 59. This passage affords a typical example of Tertullian's forced argumentation. Priests are not permitted to bury their parents; this is proved from the text in Leviticus cited in the next note. But Christians are not permitted to bury their parents; this is proved from the passages in Matt. and Luke just quoted. Therefore Christians are priests. But priests must be monogamous. Therefore all Christians must be monogamous. It is then completely inconsistent to say, as Tertullian does immediately, that the obligation to avoid defilement by avoiding contact with a corpse is not binding under the New Law — though the statement itself, of course, is true.

[101] Lev. 21. 11. This text refers exclusively to the High Priest.

[102] For the use of this expression in Tertullian, see J. C. Plumpe, *Mater Ecclesia: An Inquiry into the Concept of the Church as Mother in Early Christianity* (SCA 5, Washington 1943) 45-62.

[103] Cf. Matt. 11. 9; Luke 7. 26.

[104] Tertullian's Mariology is far from orthodox. Though he insists often and emphatically on the divine maternity and Mary's virginity *ante partum*, he does not appear to have believed that she remained a virgin *in partu* and *post partum*. Such expressions as *virgo quantum a viro, non virgo quantum a partu* and *et si virgo concepit, in partu suo nupsit* (*De carne Christi* 23), and the assumption in the same chapter that the 'brethren of Jesus' are children of Mary according to the flesh, are offensive to Catholic faith. On Tertullian's opposition to Docetism as a reason for this error, see J. C. Plumpe, 'Some Little-Known Early Witnesses to Mary's *Virginitas in Partu*,' *Theol. Stud.* 9 (1948) 568 f., and the literature there cited.

Although in the present passage the words *semel nuptura post partum* might have reference to a virginal marriage with Joseph after the birth of Christ, yet this is probably not intended since in other passages Tertullian supposes that Mary's monogamy was not virginal. He teaches here that Christ was born of a virgin espoused, but not yet married (cf. Matt. 1. 18; Luke 1. 27 and 2. 5). It is much more likely, however, that Mary and Joseph were already married when Christ was born, since they could hardly have traveled together to Bethlehem if they were not. The apparent difficulty in Luke 2. 5 is solved by reading it in the light of Matt. 1. 25. Cf. A. Edersheim, *The Life and Times of Jesus the Messiah* (New York, n. d.) 1. 155 ff.

Helvidius appealed to the authority of Tertullian in his attack on the Church's doctrine of Mary's perpetual virginity, and St. Jerome answered him very simply (*Adv. Helv.* 17): 'As to Tertullian, I have nothing else to say except that he was not a man of the Church (*Ecclesiae hominem non fuisse*).' For an excellent conspectus of Tertullian's Mariology, see J. Nissen, *Die Mariologie des heiligen Hieronymus* (Münster i. W. 1913) 24-26. Cf. also *Paradoxa Tertulliani cum Antidoto Pamelii*, in ML 1. 246 ff.

[105] Luke 2. 25.

[106] Cf. Mark 1. 30.

[107] Cf. Matt. 16. 18. In the *De pudicitia* (21), a work of his Montanist period, Tertullian declares that the power of the keys which Peter received on the occasion of his confession was a personal prerogative, though earlier (*Scorp.* 10) he had clearly stated the opposite: '*Nam etsi adhuc clausum putas caelum, memento claves eius hic dominum Petro et per eum ecclesiae reliquisse . . . .*'

[108] The word is γυνή. The text here, 1 Cor. 9. 5, has ἀδελφὴν γυναῖκα, though there is some manuscript evidence for ἀδελφὰς γυναῖκας. Tertullian and Hilary read the plural; Clement of Alexandria, Jerome, and Augustine have both singular and plural. See above, *De exhort. cast.*, n. 67.

[109] The argument is this: St. Paul asks, 'Do I not have the right to eat and drink? Do I not have the right to travel with women?' Tertullian contends that the close connection of the two sentences shows that the women in question were not wives but rather devoted assistants who accompanied the Apostles in order to care for their bodily needs.

[110] Cf. Matt. 23. 1-3.

[111] This is an excellent statement of Christ's institution of a *vivum*

magisterium in the Church: *Ipse super cathedram suam collocaret qui* . . . .

[112] Cf. Matt. 18. 1-4, 19. 13-15; Mark 10. 13-16.

[113] The reference is obscure. Possibly we are to think of those 'who have made themselves eunuchs for the kingdom of Heaven': Matt. 19. 12.

[114] Matt. 10. 16.

[115] Pliny writes in his *Natural History* (10. 52. 104) that doves . . . *coniugii fidem non · violant, communemque servant domum.* Compare Aristotle, *Hist. anim.* 9. 7; Clement of Alexandria, *Strom.* 2. 139. 4. Modern zoologists give the dove a less edifying reputation.

[116] Cf. John 4. 17 f.

[117] Cf. Matt. 17. 3; Mark 9. 3; Luke 9. 30.

[118] Luke 1. 17.

[119] Cf. Matt. 11. 19; Mark 2. 16; Luke 7. 34.

[120] Cf. John 2. 1-10. It is gratuitous to assert that this was the only wedding Christ ever attended. Tertullian is again supposing that what Scripture does not assert it denies.

[121] Matt. 19. 8.

[122] *Ibid.* 19. 6.

[123] *Ibid.* 10. 29.

[124] Cf. *Ad ux.* 1. 7 and *De exhort. cast.* 2.

[125] Tertullian's wordplay is *destruendam — restruendam.*

[126] Matt. 5. 32.

[127] The last two sentences are quite difficult and the translation follows Oehler's text: *Non et nubere legitime potest repudiata, et si quid tale commiserit sine matrimonii nomine, non capit elogium adulterii, qua adulterium in matrimonio crimen est? Deus taliter censuit citra quam homines, ut in totum, sive per nuptias sive vulgo, alterius viri admissio adulterium pronuntietur ab eo.* Kellner-Esser prefer to begin *Nam et,* and read the sentence as a declaration rather than a question. In the second sentence, with the MSS, they read *aliter,* rather than *taliter.* The passage should then be rendered somewhat as follows: 'Before the Law a divorced woman may indeed marry again; and if here she sins when she is actually not married, she does not incur the charge of adultery in the sense that we regard adultery as a crime committed in marriage. But God's judgment on this is quite different from that of man: He terms all intercourse with a second man, whether in marriage or promiscuously, adultery — without exception.'

[128] The expression is *coniunctionem signavit. Signare,* literally,

means to "place a seal upon,' 'seal'; hence to 'confirm' or 'bless.' Cf. Oehler 2. cxcviii; also *Ad ux.* 2. 8, where Tertullian says that Christian marriage is one 'upon which the blessing sets a seal.'

[129] Gen. 2. 23.

[130] Cf. Rom. 7. 1-3; 1 Cor. 7. 39.

[131] 1 Cor. 6. 18.

[132] The words *concarnare* and *concarnatio* are neologisms in Tertullian. The expression *tertiae concarnationis* is troublesome. If we construe *ne necessitas vel occasio tertiae concarnationis irrumpat* after *abstulit repudium*, we shall find it hard to say what the *secunda concarnatio* would be. Possibly nothing more is meant than that divorce is permitted in case of adultery (a *secunda concarnatio*) because if the sinful partner is not put away, the offense may be repeated as being apparently condoned. If we construe the clause with *soli causae permittens repudium*, the following interpretation might be considered: the *prima concarnatio* is the original marriage; the *secunda* is the sin of adultery; the *tertia* would be the resumption of marital relations by the innocent husband or wife after adultery has been committed and the marriage bond thus broken by one of the partners. Such a *tertia concarnatio* would be 'necessary' or 'occasioned' if the innocent partner were not permitted to separate from the guilty. Compare *Adv. Marc.* 4. 34 and *Pastor Hermae mand.* 4. 1.

[133] Dionysius of Halicarnassus, *Ant. Rom.* 2. 25, declares that no Roman took advantage of his right to divorce until Spurius Carvilius Maximus Ruga, 520 years after the foundation of the city (231 B. C.), put away his wife for barrenness.

[134] Tertullian is here opposing Christian teaching to pagan, not Montanist to Catholic. Rigault's assertion that Tertullian as a Catholic (*Ad ux.* 2. 1) permitted remarriage after divorce cannot be proved; cf. above, n. 76 to *Ad ux.*

[135] Literally, 'from whom she has heard nothing of a *repudium*, . . . to whom she has not written a *repudium.*' It is commonly said that *repudium* is the word for a divorce at the will of one party and *divortium* for a dissolution of the marriage by mutual consent; cf. Sherman, *op. cit.* 2. 76. This is contested by Zeumer, quoted in E. A. Westermarck, *The History of Human Marriage* (5th ed. New York 1922) 3. 321. It is Zeumer's view that *divortium* was the generic word for divorce of any kind, while *repudium* is used for the public act by which one spouse notified the other of his or her intention to dissolve their marriage. Cf. *Digests* 24. 2; 50. 16. 191.

It is probably safe to say that Tertullian made no important distinction between the two words.

[136] The Latin is: *Ergo perseveret in ea cum illo necesse est quem iam repudiare non poterit, ne sic quidem nuptura, si repudiare potuisset.* The expression *ne sic quidem nuptura* is ambiguous and can mean, as the translation takes it, that even if she had gotten a divorce before he died, she could not remarry after he dies. It is also possible to interpret the words in this sense: even if she had gotten a divorce before he died, she could not have then remarried, that is, before he died. This would suggest Tertullian's recognition of what we now call *separatio a mensa et thoro*; cf. above, n. 134 to the present treatise, and the statement, in the following chapter, that the Apostle would not, 'in contravention of the precept he had established earlier, permit divorced persons to remarry.'

[137] This sentence reflects Tertullian's chiliastic eschatology. For parallel passages in his writings and for references to the literature on *refrigerium* and *prima resurrectio*, see d'Alès, *op. cit.* 134; 446-48; Waszink, *op. cit.* 401; 586-93. Compare, also, above n. 91 to *De exhort. cast.*

[138] Cf. above, *De exhort. cast.* 11 and n. 92 — Concerning the early Christian concept of death as a sleep — *dormitio* — see the interesting chapter in Rush, *op. cit.* 1-22. Tertullian's language makes clear that the Christians commemorated their dead, not on their birthdays, as was the common pagan practice, but on the anniversary of their demise. For the Christian his earthly birthday — *dies natalis* — was an entrance upon the consequences of original sin; his true *dies natalis*, one worth commemorating, was the day of his death — his entrance into eternal life. This is well expressed by St. Ambrose, *De exc. Saturi* 2. 5: 'We pay no attention to the birthdays of the dead, but commemorate with great solemnity the day on which they died.' For more details and further passages, cf. F. J. Dölger, ΙΧΘΥΣ 2. 549-69; Rush, *op. cit.* 72-87.

[139] Matt. 22. 30.

[140] Cf. Matt. 16. 37 and 1 Cor. 3. 8.

[141] Cf. John 14. 2.

[142] Cf. Matt. 20. 10.

[143] Christianity does not recognize a double standard of morality. Compare the well-known expression of St. Jerome (*Epist.* 77. 3): *Apud nos, quod non licet feminis, aeque non licet viris.*

[144] Cf. Matt. 5. 28.

[145] This statement accords with the principle of Roman law that

Nuptias non concubitus, sed consensus facit; cf. *Digests* 50. 17. 30. The Church readily accepted this principle and it was given official expression in the response of Nicholas I *Ad Bulgaros* (ES 334). Cf. above, n. 73 to *De exhort. cast.*

[146] The word *sacramentum* in this context clearly retains its early classical meaning of a solemn engagement inducing serious obligations, as a soldier's oath. The whole passage affords additional evidence that marriage was not considered a mere civil ceremony in the early Church. On this subject see J. Köhne, ' Die kirchliche Eheschliessungsform in der Zeit Tertullians,' *Theol. u. Glaube* 23 (1931) 645-54; also Kolping, *op. cit.* 28 and n. 42, where among other references, he quotes the following from Lactantius, *Epit.* 61. 7: ' *Qui habet coniugem, nihil quaerat extrinsecus, sed contentus ea sola casti et inviolati cubilis sacramenta custodiat.*' Cf. above, n. 35 to *De exhort. cast.*

[147] *Illi*, that is, the ecclesiastical authorities, just mentioned, of the ' Sensualists,' or *psychici.*

[148] Matt. 5. 42; Luke 6. 30.

[149] The idea of the Church's unity is developed at considerable length and with great skill in Tertullian's treatise *De praescriptione haereticorum*; see especially ch. 19-21.

[150] 1 Cor. 7. 39. This text, so damaging to his thesis on the absolute unlawfulness of second marriage, Tertullian almost completely ignores in the *Ad uxorem* and the *De exhortatione castitatis.*

[151] Compare Eph. 1. 9 f. and ch. 5 above. The arguments used here are repeated from earlier chapters in this treatise and are also to be found in the other two treatises on marriage.

[152] Cf. Rom. 9. 7; Gal. 4. 28.

[153] A paraphrase of 1 Cor. 3. 2.

[154] 1 Cor. 7. 1-8. The quotations which follow are all from this same chapter.

[155] It is impossible to say with certainty what the reading was in the ' authentic Greek ' to which Tertullian refers. All the best manuscript evidence we have today supports the verb form of κοιμάω which he condemns, i. e. κοιμηθῇ (in the Vulgate, *dormierit*). Rigault suggests κοιμᾶται (' if he sleep,' i. e. ' if he be dead '), providing for a *change* of two syllables. Pamelius thought, less plausibly, that Tertullian speaks of a change involving the *excision* of two syllables, from ἐὰν δὲ κεκοίμηται (' if he be dead ') to ἐὰν κοιμηθῇ (' if he will have died '). The conjectures show that the meaning of the word used by Tertullian to designate the change made is itself not clear:

eversio, in the context, can convey the idea of a 'complete change' or of a 'deletion.' However this may be, he objects that the text, which should have reference only to the past (*if her husband is already dead*), has been altered in such a way that it suggests the future (*if her husband will have died*). The textual puzzle has attracted the attention of modern critics also, but it has never been really solved. Cf. de Labriolle, *La crise montaniste* 385-90; d'Alès, *op. cit.* 241.

156 Tertullian means that the popular version of the text has a general sense and that it can be understood in two ways: 'if her husband dies' — either before or after her conversion.

157 1 Cor. 7. 21.

158 *Ibid.* 7. 18, in inverted order.

159 *Ibid.* 7. 27.

160 . . . *in nova et recenti vocatione*: for the concept of the divine 'call,' 'invitation' to partake in the salvation conferred by Christianity (also illustrated in the present paragraph from St. Paul's First Epistle to the Corinthians), see the volume to follow in the series — ACW 14: St. Prosper of Aquitaine, *De vocatione omnium gentium*.

161 The point of the elaborate argument is to show that St. Paul in this text speaks of men who were widowers at the time of their conversion. This is established from the context. The conclusion is that in these circumstances, and in no others, is second marriage permitted.

162 Cf. John 17. 21; Gal. 3. 28.

163 Cf. Apoc. 1. 6 and 5. 10.

164 *Cum ad peraequationem disciplinae sacerdotalis provocamur, deponimus infulas, et pares sumus.* The words *pares sumus* are supported by the best manuscript tradition. The context, however. would seem to require *impares sumus*, and some editors have emended the text accordingly, so that it might be translated: 'When we are called upon to live up fully to the demands of sacerdotal discipline, we are unequal to the obligation.' The reading of Kellner-Esser, *partes sumus* ('und sind wir in Stufen eingeteilt'), is unreasonable only in so far as it is unnecessary. It is borrowed from Gelenius, who may or may not have had authorization for it in the *Mesnartiana* and the *Codex Masburensis*; cf. Waszink, *op. cit.* 2*. Reading *pares sumus*, it is possible to interpret the sentence as simple irony: '. . . yet we flatter ourselves that we are the compeers of priests!' It seems much more likely, however, that Tertullian is punning on the word *par*, which can mean a partner in

marriage, and the *par* which is suggested in *peraequationem*. It is this meaning of *par*, a ' mate' or ' marriage partner,' which is adopted in the present translation.

[165] Uthina was a diocese in proconsular Africa, suffragan of Carthage. About forty years after the *De monogamia* was written, a bishop Felix of Uthina is mentioned in the minutes of a Carthaginian synod meeting under the metropolitan bishop, St. Cyprian: cf. *Sent. episc. num.* LXXXVII *de haer. bapt.* 26 (261 v. Soden). — The *Lex Scantinia* is named for a tribune of the people, otherwise unknown. Juvenal, *Sat.* 2. 44, calls it a law *de nefanda Venere*, probably pederasty. Cf. also Caelius in Cicero, *Ad fam.* 8. 12. 3 *and* 8. 14. 4. See E. Weiss, 'Lex Scantinia,' RE 12 (1925) 2413.

[166] The same charge is made in the *Philosophumena* (9. 7), where Hippolytus complains that in the days of Callistus ' digamist and trigamist bishops, priests, and deacons began to be admitted into the clergy.'

[167] Strictly, *tituli disciplinae*, are titles or honorable appellations distinctive of a certain way of life. Not infrequently, however, *titulus* is almost synonymous with *genus*: cf. Waszink, *op. cit.* 110. This is the meaning adopted here.

[168] 1 Tim. 3. 2-7, with some variations. For the Greek διδακτικόν Tertullian has *docibilis*, the Vulgate, *doctor*. In 2 Tim. 2. 24, however, the Vulgate translates the same word *docibilis*. Compare also Titus 1. 6-9.

[169] 1 Tim. 5. 14.

[170] *Ibid.* 5. 11 f.

[171] Rom. 7. 2 f. Here Tertullian has *facta alii viro*, the Vulgate, *si fuerit cum alio viro*.

[172] *Ibid.* 7. 4-6, reading *mortificamini*, which Tertullian understands as an imperative, for *mortificati estis* (ἐθανατώθητε) of the Vulgate, and *mortui in quo tenebamur* where the Vulgate has *a lege mortis in qua detinebamur*. The context contains one of Tertullian's very rare references to the Church as the body of Christ. See Plumpe, *Mater Ecclesia* 51 and n. 19.

[173] This, of course, is the precise point to be proved.

[174] Cf. Acts 16. 3; Gal. 2. 4.

[175] Cf. Acts 21. 20-26. These men were Jewish converts who had taken the vow of the Nazarites. Paul joined himself to them in order to prove his respect for the Law. Cf. also Acts 18. 18. The accusation of the Asiatic Jews that Paul ' departed from Moses' was false. He taught that ceremonial observances of the Law were not

necessary, but he did not oblige Jewish converts to give up these practices. See A. Camerlynck — A. Van der Heeren, *Commentarius in Actus Apostolorum* (7th ed. Bruges 1923) 349-52.

[176] This is the theme of the entire Epistle to the Galatians. See especially 3. 1 ff.

[177] 1 Cor. 9. 22.

[178] Gal. 4. 19.

[179] Cf. Deut. 24. 1; Matt. 19. 8.

[180] Tertullian is probably thinking of Marcion's doctrine of two gods. According to this theory, Christ represented a different God than the Old Testament God of Moses. For a recent study of Marcion's dualism, see E. C. Blackman, *Marcion and his Influence* (SPCK London 1948) 66-80.

[181] *Expugnare* indicates, classically, a completed assault. Here, however, it appears to have the force of *oppugnare*, as frequently in Tertullian and late Latin writers. Cf. Waszink, *op. cit.* 406.

[182] Cf. John 16. 12 f.

[183] Matt. 26. 41. The text is also used in *Ad mart.* (4), where it is applied with much more sympathy and understanding than in the present passage.

[184] Matt. 19. 12.

[185] Cf. Matt. 19. 16-22; Mark 10. 17-22; Luke 18. 18-24.

[186] *Nec ideo duritia imputabitur Christo de arbitrii cuiuscumque liberi vitio.* For Tertullian's teaching on grace and free will, see d'Alès, *op. cit.* 268 ff. Compare n. 73 to *Ad ux.*

[187] Deut. 30. 15; cf. Ecclus. 15. 18.

[188] It is worth noting that Catholics in Tertullian's day made the same two charges against him which Catholics make today, harshness and heresy. — For the Latin loan word *haeresis* (αἵρεσις), cf. H. Janssen, *Kultur u. Sprache. Zur Geschichte der alten Kirche im Spiegel der Sprachentwicklung von Tertullian bis Cyprian* (Lat. christ. prim. 8, Nijmegen 1938) 110-35; H. Schlier, TWNT 1 (1933) 180-84. The word meaning literally a 'taking,' a 'choice,' was used, for a long period of time, to designate a 'doctrine' or 'school,' e. g. of philosophers (similarly, the Latin *secta,* 'sect'). The connotation of a 'school' of doctrine continues when the word is applied (e. g. by Josephus) to religious factions among the Jews, and when Ignatius of Antioch uses it (e. g. *Trall.* 6. 1) as a technical term in a wholly pejorative sense: a doctrine professed by Christians in opposition to Christian orthodoxy.

[189] Cf. 1 Tim. 4. 3.

[190] . . . *in proelio*: cf. above, n. 95, *De exhort. cast.*

[191] Cf. Matt. 24. 13.

[192] In the *De pudicitia* (5 and 22), another Montanist treatise, Tertullian uses a similar *a fortiori* argument to prove that adultery should not be pardoned by ecclesiastical authority.

[193] The heretic Hermogenes was one of Tertullian's favorite targets. He was a contemporary, who had come from the East and settled at Carthage where he was a painter of some prominence. In the East, Theophilus of Antioch wrote a treatise against him: cf. Eusebius, *Hist. eccl.* 4. 24. For a detailed refutation of his dualism and his errors on creation and the soul, see especially Tertullian's *Adversus Hermogenem* and the *De anima*. The *De censu animae*, a treatise in which Tertullian attacks the materialism of Hermogenes, has been lost; cf. Waszink, *op. cit.* 7*-14*. Tertullian repeatedly refers to his abuse of marriage. In *Adv. Hermog.* 1 he calls him *totus adulter* and says, *nubit assidue*.

[194] The clause may also be translated: '. . . whence (*unde* of illation) he presumes that even the soul is material' (thus Thelwall). It seems better, however, in view of the actual doctrine of Hermogenes, to read *unde* closely with *materia*, i. e. '. . . matter, whence he presumes the soul to be derived.' His fundamental error dealt with the origin (*de censu*) of the soul and only *per consequens* did he misrepresent its nature. In the *De anima* (11) Tertullian writes: *Ceterum adversus Hermogenem, qui eam ex materia, non ex dei flatu contendit, flatum proprie tuemur.*

[195] See above, n. 2.

[196] Cf. Matt. 6. 25-32 and parallel passages there indicated.

[197] D'Alès, *op. cit.* 474 n. 5, sees here a sarcastic reference to persons who approved of flight during the time of persecution. The words, *homini ad fugam proximo*, might also be interpreted of flight on the Day of Judgment, a sense which is suggested by the assertion that the time for flight is near at hand. This interpretation finds support in the consideration that the objections in this chapter follow closely those urged in *Ad ux.* 1. 4 f., where the idea of the proximate parousia is strong.

[198] *Habet viduam utique, quam assumat licebit. Non unam generis huius uxorem, sed etiam plures habere concessum.* Kellner-Esser mistakenly render this as a sarcastic statement by Tertullian, probably interpreting it as a reference to the laxity of the 'Psychics.' We have here, however, a close parallel to the passage in *De exhort. cast.* 12, where Tertullian, in answering a similar argument pro-

posed in favor of second marriage, says that a widower may take one of the widows of the Church to be a spiritual wife, adding: ' Huiusmodi uxores etiam plures haberi deo gratum est.' The reference in both places is very probably to the practice of living with the so-called *mulieres subintroductae*. This extraordinary practice seems to have existed from a very early period in the Church's history. Two forms are usually referred to: the communal life of ascetics of both sexes, who lived together under the same roof; and the very dubious relationship between a member of the clergy and a woman, quite commonly one of the consecrated virgins of the Church, who lived in the same house with him, under the plea of spiritual relationship. Tertullian, apparently, saw nothing wrong with the practice as it existed in his day, but objections to it are frequent and vigorous from the middle of the third century on, both in Church councils and in the writings of such Fathers as Cyprian, Jerome, Basil, Gregory of Nyssa, Gregory Nazianzen, and Chrysostom. Cf. H. Achelis, *Virgines subintroductae. Ein Beitrag zu I Kor. VII* (Leipzig 1902) esp. 12-20; P. de Labriolle, 'Le mariage spirituel dans l'antiquité chrétienne,' *Rev. hist.* 137 (1921) 204-225. For additional literature, cf. J. Sickenberger, ' Syneisakten,' LTK 9 (1937) 943.

[199] Cf. Gen. 19. 26. It is difficult to see the precise point of the comparison. Perhaps nothing more is intended than the insinuation that in both cases an undisciplined urge leads to the violation of God's command.

[200] See n. 2 to *Ad uxorem* for some of the disabilities imposed by the *Lex Iulia*. The law required that widows, widowers, and divorced persons should remarry or suffer the penalties imposed on the celibate. These penalties endured until the time of Constantine, and it is quite likely that the influence of Christian ideals brought about their ultimate abrogation. This is the only place in his writings where Tertullian hints at the difficulty such civil legislation would cause Christians who wished to practice the continence he recommended.

[201] Quoted from Isa. 22. 13 and 1 Cor. 15. 32.

[202] Cf. Matt. 24. 19. Tertullian understands Christ's discourse as referring to the destruction of Jerusalem by the Romans as well as to the devastation of the world on the last day.

[203] Compare the harsh realism of these lines with similar passages in *Ad ux.* 1. 5 and *De exhort. cast.* 9.

[204] John the Baptist, rather than John the Apostle; cf. above, ch. 8.

[205] Cf. Judith 16. 26.

[206] Possibly a secondary allusion to the judges before whom the Christians appeared during the persecutions. Most of the examples which follow have been used before. See especially *Ad ux.* 1. 6 f. and *De exhort. cast.* 13.

[207] The reference may be to some pagan custom resembling the former practice of suttee in India or to such classical cases as that of Evadne (Euripides, *Suppl.* 980 ff.), and the three widows mentioned by Pausanias 4. 2. 7.

[208] Fortuna was a Roman goddess venerated under many titles, originally regarded as a bringer of good fortune, but later as a deity of chance or luck. As a goddess of women (*Muliebris*), she was closely associated with the goddess of light and birth, *Mater Matuta*, here mentioned with her. The feast of both was celebrated on the same day, June 11. The fact that only a monogamist woman could come in contact with her statue, is also mentioned by Dionysius of Halicarnassus (8. 56. 4) and others. Cf. G. Wissowa, *op. cit.* 258.

[209] One of the most ancient Roman divinities, bearing an intimate relationship with the god of openings and beginnings, Janus. Cf. Wissowa, *ibid.* 110 f.; W. W. Fowler, *The Roman Festivals* (London 1916) 154-57; also the note immediately preceding.

[210] See *De exhortatione castitatis* n. 106.

[211] Possibly to be identified with the Artemis of Tauris in the Chersonese.

[212] The Pythia was the priestess of Apollo who uttered the prophetic responses at Delphi. During its period of greatest prosperity there were three prophetesses in attendance at the shrine. They were virgins of honorable birth, in early times young girls but, at a later period, women over fifty. Πυθώ was the early name of Delphi and its surroundings.

[213] Cf. Rom. 13. 14; Gal. 3. 27.

[214] The expression is . . . *de paradiso sanctitatis.* It is interesting to compare the *Summa theologica* Iᵃ. 98. 1 f., where St. Thomas refers to and refutes earlier writers (including Gregory of Nyssa, *De hom. opif.* 17) who said that *in statu innocentiae generatio prolis non fuisset per coitum.* In the *De anima* (38. 2) Tertullian declares that when men reach puberty, concupiscence brings them forth *de paradiso integritatis.* It is not perfectly clear, however, that these expressions are to be understood as implying that there was no use of sex in the garden of Eden before the fall; but cf. above, n. 56.

[215] Suggesting St. Paul's use of the phrase in 1 Cor. 15. 22.

INDEX

INDEX

Aalders, G. J. D., 143
Aaron, 82
abortion, 17, 61, 119, 147 f.
Abraham, 80 ff., 140, 156
abrenuntiatio, 117
abrogation, of Old Law, 52, 79, 83, 101 f.
absolute goodness, 12 f., 47 f., 54 f., 73 f.
abstinence, periodic, 58
abuse, of marriage, 70; of Scripture, 97
Achaean Juno, 19, 63, 108
Achelis, H., 169
Adam, first, 108; ecstatic vision, 134, 137; father of human race, 44; married before the fall, 155; a monogamist, 11, 50 f., 76 f.; restoration to Paradise, 79; sin of, 44 f.; Second, 80, 108; a third, 108
Adam, K., 140
adeo, 141
adjuration of demon, 58
adulterer, adulteress, 56, 94, 101, 112 ·
adultery, 27, 28, 143, 148; definition of, 93, 104; identified with any pluralism in marriage, 87; an unpardonable sin, 141, 168; animals not born of, 77 f.
advocate, the Paraclete, 76
advocatus, 153
aeneum spiculum, 119
affectare, 123
affection, a conjugal obligation, 91

affinity, impediment of, 84, 158
African Ceres, 19, 63
Agar, 156
age, an adornment, 60
Agobardinus, Codex, 116, 126, 127, 130, 144
d'Alès, A., 41, 115, 116, 122, 124, 126, 132, 134, 136, 138, 139, 141, 145, 153, 158, 163, 165
aliquis, 149
allegory, 115
alms, 35
Alpha and Omega, 78 ff., 155
altar, 20, 59, 60, 122
ambition, 14
Ambrose, St., *De Abr.* 1. 9: 125; *De exc. Saturi* 2. 5: 163; *De myst.* 6. 31-33: 128; *De sacr.* 3. 1: 128; *Epist.* 1: 129; 38. 6: 118
Ammonites, 158
angelorum candidati, 131
angels, 11, 15, 17; witnesses at Christian marriage, 35
anger, 91
anima, animus, 146
animals, monogamy of, 77 f., 87
Anna, daughter of Phanuel, 86; wife of Elcana, 148
annihilation, 92
annual sacrifice, for the dead, 59 f., 92, 146
ἄνθρωπος πνευματικός, ψυχικός, 151
Antichrist, 107
Apis, 149
Apollo, 63, 108, 170
Apologists, 119, 128

173

ANCIENT CHRISTIAN WRITERS

The Works of the Fathers in Translation

Edited by

J. QUASTEN, S. T. D., and J. C. PLUMPE, Ph. D.